D0371628

WOMEN INVENTORS

A M E R I C A N
P R O F I L E S

WOMEN INVENTORS

■

Linda Jacobs Altman

✓®
Facts On File, Inc.

Women Inventors

Copyright © 1997 by Linda Jacobs Altman

All rights reserved. No part of this book may be reproduced or utilized in any form or by any means, electronic or mechanical, including photocopying, recording, or by any information storage or retrieval systems, without permission in writing from the publisher. For information contact:

Facts On File, Inc.
132 West 31st Street
New York NY 10001

Library of Congress Cataloging-in-Publication Data

Altman, Linda Jacobs, 1943–.
    Women inventors / Linda Jacobs Altman.
        p. cm.—(American profiles)
    Includes bibliographical references and index.
    ISBN 0-8160-3385-4
    1. Women inventors—United States—Biography. 2. Inventions—
United States—History. I. Title. II. Series: American profiles
(Facts On File, Inc.)
    T39.A54   1997
    609′.2′273—dc20   96-20460
    [B]

Facts On File books are available at special discounts when purchased in bulk quantities for businesses, associations, institutions, or sales promotions. Please call our Special Sales Department in New York at 212/967-8800 or 800/322-8755.

You can find Facts On File on the World Wide Web at http://www.factsonfile.com

Text design by Ron Monteleone

Cover design by Matt Galemmo

Printed in the United States of America

MP FOF 10 9 8 7 6

This book is printed on acid-free paper.

Contents

LIBRARY
DEXTER SCHOOLS
DEXTER, NM 88230

Introduction

*I*n July 1995, the National Inventors Hall of Fame celebrated the grand opening of Inventure Place, the hall's beautiful new facility in Akron, Ohio. The dedication ceremony on July 20 launched a weekend of events that included conferences, guided tours of the hall—even a block party with "live music, food, fun, and dancing in the streets." Seven new members were inducted. One of the seven was Dr. Stephanie Kwolek, the DuPont chemist who invented Kevlar, a synthetic fiber strong enough to stop bullets.

The history of the process of invention has been written mostly by and about men. Only in the last decades of the twentieth century has the inventive output of women begun to receive the attention it deserves. Invention is the product of an inquiring mind and an active imagination—qualities that women possess and use as well as men.

According to studies on human creativity, invention is a three-stage process: recognizing the problem, defining the solution, then creating a process or device capable of putting that solution into practice. The typical inventor likes to tinker: to combine and recombine an assemblage of parts into new, even startling, forms. This ability to look at problems with an inventive eye often shows itself at an early age.

No one knows how many talented women inventors have been lost to gender stereotyping. Those who succeeded had to be tough as well as creative, able to overcome numerous obstacles along the way. One of the most formidable of those obstacles is the patent application, which is both complicated and expensive. To qualify for a patent, an inventor must prove three things to the satisfaction of the patent examiners: that she is its creator, that the device or process is new, and that it is useful.

The patent process begins with a preliminary disclosure statement in which the applicant furnishes a sketch of the device along with an explanation of how it works and a statement detailing the ways in which it meets the criteria of novelty and usefulness. The statement must be signed by two witnesses in the presence of a notary public and filed with the U.S. Patent Office. The disclosure establishes priority in case someone else should come up with the same idea before a patent can be granted. This is a crucial precaution in a field where the difference between success and failure depends upon who is first to file.

After the disclosure comes the patent search, an exhaustive records check to make sure the invention is not a duplicate of an earlier one. Most successful applicants use the services of an experienced patent attorney to plow through the morass of details and regulations and to write the application in the exact format required by the Patent Office. Final approval usually takes around two years, and the process can cost several thousand dollars in legal fees and other expenses.

Despite the difficulties, inventors of both sexes have prized the designation "U.S. Patent No. such-and-such," which validates their creations as unique and worthwhile. This official recognition has been particularly important to women, whose work has too often been ignored or denigrated.

In 1990, the U.S. Patent Office celebrated its 200th anniversary with a special exhibit on women inventors, entitled "Woman's Place Is in the Patent Office." Professor Fred Amram of the University of Minnesota assembled a collection of memorabilia that surprised many people with its variety and richness. The exhibit attracted new attention to the accomplishments of women inventors.

The following year, the Inventors Hall of Fame elected its first female member, Dr. Gertrude Elion, creator of the antileukemia drug Purinethol. "I may be the first woman in the Hall of Fame," Elion said in her acceptance speech, "but I know that I certainly won't be the last." She was right. Elizabeth Hazen and Rachel Brown, creators of the fungicidal drug

Nystatin, were inducted in 1994; Stephanie Kowlek, previously mentioned, was inducted in 1995.

The women profiled in these pages have distinguished themselves with inventions ranging from biotech to Barbie dolls. Some, such as Hazen, Brown, and physicist Katharine Blodgett, were scientists engaged in well-defined research. Others were "accidental inventors" who created a new process or device as a by-product of their efforts to solve a problem.

Dr. Josephine Baker was a public health physician trying to improve health care when she created her measured-dosage eyedropper. Carrie Everson wanted to save her gold-speculating husband from financial ruin when she began tinkering with her ore separation process. Amanda Theodosia Jones followed what she called a "psychic vision" when she devised her vacuum canning process.

Inventors with a knack for promotion sometimes went on to become entrepreneurs. Madam C. J. Walker, Ida Rosenthal, Bette Graham, and Ruth Handler parlayed their inventions into successful companies, and became millionaires in the bargain.

These inventors come from different times, different places, different backgrounds, yet they all share one thing: they have been creators and achievers in spite of social barriers against them. In the process, they have built a foundation for future generations of inventive women who want to be judged by their work rather than by their gender.

Amanda Theodosia Jones
(1835–1914)

*T*he creativity that motivates inventors to tinker with new devices and dream up new processes is not different from that which inspires writers, artists, and other original thinkers. All share the ability to link intellect and imagination to bring something new into the world. While some creative people have more-or-less ordinary personal lives, others develop quirky interests and behave in ways that seem downright odd.

By modern standards, Amanda Theodosia Jones belongs in the second group. Many inventors have credited their ideas to dreams; Jones believed that hers came from a spirit. She was a true American original: teacher, poet, spiritualist, and inventor. By anyone's standards, Amanda Jones packed a lot of living into her seventy-eight years and helped to shape the food processing industry in the bargain.

Amanda Theodosia Jones was born on October 19, 1835, in the small town of East Bloomfield, New York, the fourth of twelve children born to Henry and Mary Mott Jones. She was the precocious child of a book-loving family: "Books," she said in her autobiography, "were more necessary than daily bread to our parents." At the age of seven, when most children were still reading primers, Amanda plunged into the *English Reader*, a high-school level anthology of literary classics.

Her imagination was as formidable as her intellect. When she was only eight years old, she found a lost key for her mother after a "spirit voice" told her where to look. That was the first of many occasions when dreams, visions, or voices would guide her actions. Her autobiography, written when she was in her seventies, mentions dozens of such incidents.

1

Throughout history, many creative people have felt that their best ideas came from outside themselves. The ancient Greeks believed that nine goddesses, called "muses," presided over the arts and sciences. Greek artists usually explained the origin of their best ideas with a single phrase: "The muse was upon me." Nineteenth-century spiritualists credited their ideas to spirit guides. During Amanda Jones' lifetime, interest in supernatural phenomena was strong. Though the vast majority censured spiritualism as anything from simple foolishness to outright heresy, many people sincerely believed that they could communicate with "the other side" or learn the shape of the future through prophetic dreams.

Amanda Theodosia Jones was one of these people. At the age of thirteen, this bright, imaginative girl had an experience that confirmed her belief in psychic phenomena and changed the shape of her life. One day at school, her beloved older brother, Lester, collapsed and died before her eyes, victim of a heart defect. In her shock and grief, she connected his death to a dream she'd had two years earlier. In retrospect, she was sure the dream had been prophetic. Two years before her brother died, Amanda Jones dreamt that

> Lester and I were walking, hand in hand, upon a lonely road. At my right . . . ran the edge of a sheer precipice. At his left was a dense, dark forest. [Lester said] "Someone is there who has followed me a long time. He is following me now. I can never escape from him. When he comes to take me I must go."[1]

The experience devastated the impressionable teenager, who escaped the pain of a life she couldn't control by retreating into her beloved books. By the age of fifteen, she was alternating between teaching at a backwoods school and continuing her own high school education in town. Such an arrangement wasn't unusual at the time. In 1850, a basic education consisted of eight grades; only a handful of academically gifted students went on to high school. Most found jobs or apprenticed themselves to

---

[1]Amanda T. Jones, *A Psychic Autobiography* (1910; reprint, New York: Arno Publishing Co., 1980), 39.

skilled workmen to learn a trade. Teachers didn't need college degrees or credentials; a good grasp of the "three Rs" and a knack for helping others to learn was qualification enough.

Amanda Jones certainly had the first of those requirements, but there is nothing to indicate whether she had the second. Her autobiography states that she became a teacher at fifteen but says little about the work itself or how she liked it.

At seventeen, she had what was described as a "physical breakdown" that left her a virtual invalid for six years. Some people believe that this breakdown was a clinical depression, brought on by Amanda's inability to cope with the reality of her brother's death. The description of symptoms in her autobiography suggests the possibility of chronic tuberculosis. Whatever the nature of the illness, it was disabling.

For the rest of her life, Amanda's health would be what people in those days described as "delicate." She became a patron of various spas that offered treatments ranging from mineral cures to compressed-air baths, and she immersed herself in spiritualist beliefs and practices. During her convalescence, Jones published a steady stream of poetry, most of it abstract and "otherworldly," with just the right touch of Victorian moralizing to make it appealing to general audiences.

Reality intruded on this private world in 1861, with the beginning of the Civil War. Three days after the first shot was fired at Fort Sumter, Jones wrote one of her most impassioned narrative poems, a scathing indictment of war, filled with brutal, often gruesome, images of its horrors. Amanda Jones' horror over the Civil War is captured in one of her most powerful poems, "The Prophesy of the Dead." Its last stanza reads:

> *When the foes of the nation have pressed*
> *To its lips the sponge reeking in gall,*
> *When the spear has gone into the breasts*
>
> *And the skies have been rent by its call,*
> *It shall rise from its rest:*
> *It shall rise and shall rule over all.*[2]

---

[2]Ibid., 103.

Later, she wrote a series of "war songs," which saw publication in *Frank Leslie's Weekly*. These verses glorified the Union cause and the heroism of the struggle. For Amanda Jones, there was no contradiction between these martial verses and her earlier antiwar poem. To her way of thinking, it was perfectly possible to despise war, while still believing in the cause that inspired an army to fight.

On a practical level, Jones seems to have handled the war and its aftermath by escaping to the countryside of upstate New York. From 1861 to 1869, she lived twenty miles outside of Buffalo, writing her verses, communing with her "spirit friends," and gathering her strength for a return to the wider world.

In the summer of 1869, Jones had what she considered a prophetic dream, which left her with the unshakable conviction that it was time to move on to new challenges. A few weeks later, she accepted an editorial job on the staff of a popular farmer's publication called *Western Rural*. This was followed by a stint as editor of a children's magazine, *The Bright Side*.

In 1872, while still supporting herself as a writer and editor, Jones got the idea that was to lead to her vacuum canning process. Exactly where it came from, she never said. Creative people often don't know the source of their ideas. Perhaps this is why they so often invoke dreams, muses, or helpful spirits to explain their breakthrough ideas.

Considering Amanda Jones' beliefs, it would hardly be surprising for her to credit her invention to the guidance of spirits. Instead, she made a point of stating that the concept was entirely her own. She insisted that she dozed off during one of her air baths, and woke with the idea for vacuum canning firmly in mind.

Jones had never canned a jar of fruit in her life, nor had she ever shown the slightest interest in machinery. Aware of her lack of mechanical ability or scientific training, she wrote Leroy C. Cooley in Albany, New York. Some accounts describe Cooley as Jones' cousin, while others call him an in-law.

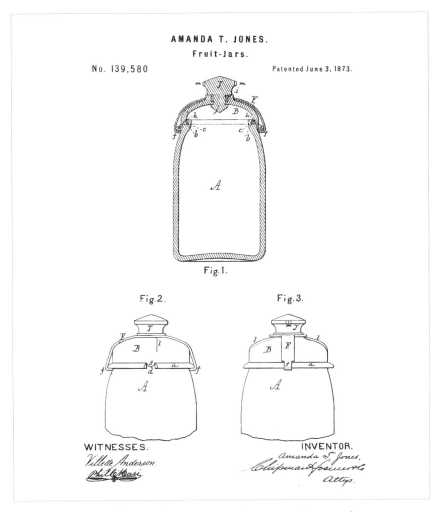

Amanda Jones' vacuum canning process became the
cornerstone of one of the most unusual business experiments in
American history.
(The Woman's Canning and Preserving Company)

Amanda herself identified him as "my sister's husband's cousin." He was apparently a scientist who possessed the technical knowledge that she lacked. Amanda Jones maintained that she woke from a nap with these exact words in her mind:

I see how fruit can be canned without cooking it. The air must be exhausted from the cells and fluid made to take its place. The fluid must be airless also—a light syrup of sugar and water—that, or the juice of fruit.[3]

Although Cooley was somewhat put off by her ardent spiritualism, he saw merit in her idea, and agreed to help develop it. Canning had been around since 1810, when a candy maker and distiller named Nicolas-François Appert answered the call of the French army for foodstuffs that could be easily transported and kept for long periods by troops in the field. Appert put up soups, fruits, vegetables, and other foodstuffs in glass jars reinforced with wire. About the same time, Englishman Peter Durand created the tin can for the Royal Navy.

The flaw that limited canned goods to military and other emergency use was taste. Existing methods required that food be well cooked. The result was a loss of both flavor and texture. Modern nutritionists have since learned that food also lost most of its nutritive value. It was the idea of canning uncooked, flavorful foods that made Amanda Jones' concept attractive. If that could be accomplished, canning would become a commercially viable process. Jones envisioned an enormous industry, conducting "a traffic in the very means of life."

She and Cooley set to work. They started with grapes, largely because they were readily available at that time of year. Though early efforts failed to achieve a vacuum seal on the jars, the partners refused to give up. They felt certain there was a way to expel air from the jars.

After many trials, they hit upon a process that involved steaming the sealed jars to raise the internal temperature to 120 degrees Fahrenheit. This did not cook the fruit, but it did cause the contents of the jars to expand, forcing out the air. A test batch canned in this way kept for more than five weeks.

Triumphant over their achievement, Jones and Cooley applied for and received a process patent. That was only the

---

[3]Ibid., 339.

beginning of their work; they received a total of seven patents in 1873 alone.

The next step was to arrange financing and begin production. This proved to be a long and difficult process for Jones, whose frail health and ardent spiritualism left her ill-equipped for the rough and tumble world of American business.

Though she lacked the talent to become an entrepreneur, her experiments with canning had revealed an unexpected mechanical ability. That in turn led to one of the strangest episodes in her remarkable life. A Pennsylvania oil man asked her to create a burner mechanism that could safely utilize crude oil for fuel. All existing burners were dangerous to use and impossible to regulate. Intrigued, Jones went to the oil fields of western Pennsylvania to study the problem.

Her solution was a simple safety valve that controlled the amount of oil released from the holding tank—an innovation that the U.S. Navy hailed as the breakthrough that could allow its ships to use oil instead of coal for fuel. Jones patented her "Safety Burner" on March 23, 1880. Shortly thereafter a wealthy financier offered her a lucrative contract to produce and market the burner. The project was barely under way when the investor lost his fortune in stock speculation, leaving Jones to carry on by herself. Once more thrust unprepared into the business world, she couldn't capitalize on the commercial value of her invention and was forced to abandon it.

By 1890, she had returned to the canning enterprise and had devised a way of turning it into a profitable business that would also serve her philosophical ideals. The women's rights movement was in full swing, demanding that women be able to vote, hold property in their own names, sign contracts, and enter business agreements. Amanda Jones didn't consider herself a feminist, but as an unmarried woman she was painfully aware of the difficulties a woman faced if she was without the protection of a man. She proposed to establish a company where women would be able to earn their way with dignity. All executives, employees, and even stockholders would be women.

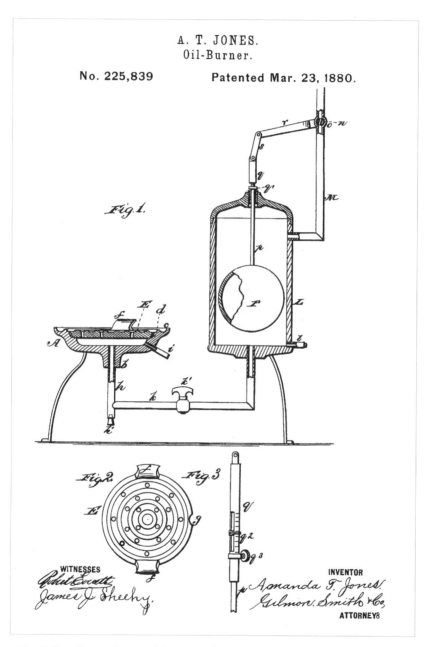

A. T. JONES.
Oil-Burner.

No. 225,839

Patented Mar. 23, 1880.

Fig. 1.

Fig. 2.   *Fig. 3.*

WITNESSES

INVENTOR

ATTORNEYS

The Safety Burner invented by Amanda Jones attracted attention from the U.S. Navy but never made it into production. She continued to defend the soundness of her design until the end of her life.

Because the Chicago meatpacking industry had shown interest in her vacuum process, she incorporated the Woman's Canning and Preserving Company in that city. At the beginning, the only two men involved in the company were Leroy C. Cooley and a boilerman named Mike. Amanda Jones sold the stock, hired the executives, and even trained the workers. The company showed every sign of thriving. Not three months after it opened for business, the biggest jobber in New York City placed an order for 24,000 cases. "We paid our bills, and throve, and won respect," Jones said. This early success satisfied her completely; it only made the rest of the executives and stockholders greedy for more.

The company president proposed to admit a group of male investors, who had agreed to put up $80,000 and manage the company's business affairs in return for half the profits. Against her better judgment, Jones went along with the arrangement. The entry of these outside investors was the beginning of the end for her. The company lost its character as a woman's business and resorted to sharp sales tactics to induce people to buy its stocks. Within three years, a heartbroken Amanda was forced out of the company she had founded, once more the victim of her own rarefied ideals. That was 1893, and though Jones would live for an additional twenty-one years, the details of her life become hazy.

Her autobiography, published in 1910, is short on facts and long on symbolism in the final chapters. After an impassioned description of how she lost control of the company, Jones talked about barren hills and purified gold, about guiding spirits, prophesies, and the speech of seraphim. In the concluding paragraphs, she seemed to be rehearsing her own death with a melancholy eulogy and a final farewell.

Her actual death occurred in 1914, at the age of seventy-eight. Though her invention brought neither wealth nor fame, her canning process became the foundation for a multimillion-dollar industry that affects the lives—and the dietary habits—of people all over the world.

Chronology

October 19, 1835	born in East Bloomfield, New York
1848	brother dies suddenly of heart disease
1850	begins teaching in a backwoods school
1852	physical "breakdown"
1854	sells poem to *Ladies' Repository* magazine
1861	publishes first book, *Ulah, and Other Poems*
	writes "The Prophesy of the Dead"
	writes Civil War songs for *Frank Leslie's Weekly*
1867	publishes anthology, *Poems*
1872	dreams canning process
	writes Leroy C. Cooley
1873	with Cooley, patents vacuum canning process
1880	patents oil burner
1890	founds Woman's Canning and Preserving Company
1893	forced out of the company
1910	publishes *A Psychic Autobiography*
1914	dies at the age of seventy-eight

Further Reading

Braude, Ann. *Radical Spirits: Spiritualism and Women's Rights in Nineteenth-Century America*. Boston: Beacon Press, 1989. Does not discuss Jones directly, but supplies an excellent overview of her spiritualist beliefs.

Jones, Amanda Theodosia. *A Psychic Autobiography*. New York: Greaves Publishing Co., 1910. Reprint, Arno Publishing Co. *Signal Lives* Series, 1980. Jones' story, told in her own words, with an emphasis on her spiritualist beliefs.

Macdonald, Anne L. *Feminine Ingenuity: Women and Invention in America*. New York: Ballantine Books, Inc., 1992. Sections on Amanda Jones as inventor of vacuum canning process and safety oil burner.

Vare, Ethlie Ann and Greg Ptacek. *Mothers of Invention*. New York: William Morrow and Co., 1988. Brief mention of Jones.

Carrie Everson
(1842–1914)

Carrie Everson's husband wasn't the only one infected with gold fever. People came to Colorado from all points east, with "Pikes Peak or Bust" signs on their wagons.
(Courtesy Denver Public Library, Western History Department)

*M*ining is one of those human activities that is part worka-day technology and part romantic legend. On the one hand, it is a basic industry that produces raw materials to supply dozens of other industries. On the other hand, it is—or at least was—a massive treasure hunt that attracted dreamers, schemers, and scoundrels of all kinds.

Carrie Everson became involved with mining in the days of the Colorado gold rush, when wagons lumbered west sporting "Pikes Peak or Bust" signs and fast-talking promoters sold shares in dubious mining ventures. Her oil flotation process for mining low-grade ore was a good system that suffered from bad timing and Everson's own retiring nature.

Not until her patent had expired did the industry discover the true value of oil flotation mining. It could transform a tapped-out mine into a productive one by extracting valuable metals or minerals from low-grade ore.

The story of the remarkable inventor who gave the flotation process to the mining industry is a puzzle to delight the hearts of any mystery fan, neatly divided between facts that can be verified or at least corroborated and legends that won't die. Sources seem to agree on at least three things: Everson patented the oil flotation system in her own name, disappeared from Colorado around 1909, and in 1915, became the object of an intensive search by the Colorado Scientific Society.

The flotation process itself has been hailed as a breakthrough technology that helped transform mining from a highly speculative activity into a thriving and profitable industry. For this achievement, the Scientific Society intended to honor Everson with "a fortune if she is living, or some lasting form of memorial if she is dead."

Carrie Jane Billings was born on August 27, 1842, near Sharon, Massachusetts. Little is known of her parents or her early life, except that the family moved to Springfield, Illinois, in 1851 and saw to it that Carrie received a good education. In 1864, she married prominent Chicago physician William Knight Everson.

Those who knew Carrie Everson described her as an unassuming, soft-spoken woman who was not particularly assertive or adept in dealing with people but who possessed a fine mind and the ability to think a problem through. For more than twelve years, she lived the normal life of a matron of comfortable circumstances. She tended to her home, bore five children, and kept up her intellectual interests in the free moments she could squeeze from her busy schedule.

Whether by accident or design, Everson limited her studies to subjects that had some bearing on her daily life. In this way, she was able to indulge her passion for learning without appearing "unfeminine." When her husband was building his reputation as a doctor, she studied medicine and chemistry. When he invested in Colorado mining stocks, she took up mineralogy.

It was this involvement with mining that ultimately changed her life. Around 1878, William Everson met promoter Mark M. "Brick" Pomeroy, who offered what seemed to be the investment of a lifetime: a gold mine in Colorado. Pomeroy was basically a charming and thoroughly persuasive con man who had a gift for turning otherwise intelligent people into victims of his schemes and dreams. He convinced Dr. Everson to invest $40,000 in the Golden Age Mining Company, a paper corporation that never sank a mine shaft or dug an honest ounce of gold.

> *Through [his newspaper columns] Pomeroy in that fatherly, persuasive style which made him so famous . . . placed before the eyes of his Eastern and Southern readers such wonderful tales of the fabulous wealth lying within the depths of these mountains . . . that for months and months the coin of the realm poured into his coffers in an almost ceaseless stream, averaging thousands of dollars daily.* [1]

Before Pomeroy was through, he had reduced the Eversons from a life of comfortable prosperity to one of near poverty. Soon after the investment soured, they picked up the pieces of their lives and moved to Denver, apparently to see if anything could be salvaged from their ill-advised adventure. Another reason may have been Dr. Everson's failing health.

At that time, Denver was well known as a sanctuary for seriously ill people. Its clean, dry, mountain air was considered to be a tonic for invalids, especially those with tuberculosis and other lung diseases. In the late 1800s, this "one-lung army," as they were called, numbered 30,000 people: one-fifth of Denver's population.

---

[1] "'Brick' Pomeroy in Denver." *The Denver Times*. September 9, 1900, p. 36.

Carrie Everson

The nature of Dr. Everson's affliction is unknown, but the search for a cure occupied a great deal of his time and energy. In the early 1880s, that search took him all the way to Mexico. While he was gone, Carrie began her experiments in oil flotation, drawing upon her years of study in chemistry and mineralogy to develop the process that would one day revolutionize mining.

At this point in the strange story of Carrie Everson, fact and legend have a parting of the ways. According to one account that was widely accepted for many years, Everson was a Denver schoolteacher who accidentally discovered the basic principle of flotation while washing ore sacks for her assayer brother.

She was scrubbing a particularly greasy sack when she noticed something interesting: the dross (waste matter) floated in the oily water, while the flakes of gold settled to the bottom. From that clue, she developed her process. This version of the story easily captured the public imagination, with its flavor of old western storytellers, spinning their yarns by campfire light. It also offered a plausible explanation of how a modest, properly "feminine" woman could have invented something so technical.

The legend of the schoolteacher and the ore sack was partly responsible for Everson becoming lost; when the Colorado Scientific Society first set out to find her, they were looking for someone who didn't exist: a spinster schoolteacher with a brother who worked in the assayer's office.

> In the search [for Carrie Everson] . . . the assertion that [she was] 'Miss Carrie J. Everson," and that she was a Denver school teacher, led the investigators on the wrong scent. . . . The Denver school records . . . showed no "Miss Everson." Then it was found that the inventor was married, and that she was a nurse instead of a school teacher.[2]

The real Carrie Everson was a thorough researcher who tested and retested her procedures until she was satisfied that they performed correctly. By the time her husband returned from

---

[2]Arthur Chapman. "Mother of New Gold Treating Process Lost." *The Denver Times* November 12, 1915, 1.

15

Mexico, she had a workable oil floatation process. What she didn't have was the ability to deal with the rigors of patenting her work. William stepped in to help with that dreaded procedure, and on August 24, 1886, Carrie J. Everson received patent number 348,157 for "Process of Concentrating Ores."

Some believed that William Everson, and not his wife, had the original idea for the process and that Carrie developed it under his constant supervision. The Eversons' son John debunked that claim when the Colorado Scientific Society interviewed him in 1915. He clearly recalled his mother's experiments during the time his father was away in Mexico. To many who have tried to unravel the story of Carrie Everson, the most compelling argument for acknowledging her as the sole inventor is not John Everson's testimony, but the fact that Carrie patented the process in her name alone.

Everyone who knew Carrie Everson agreed that she was honest to a fault, and so self-effacing that she tended to minimize her own achievements, not inflate them. It would have been out of character for her to claim undue credit for anything.

For two years, the Eversons tried to interest local mining companies in Carrie's invention. Nobody cared about a process for extracting precious metals from low-grade ore when there was gold enough for everyone, just waiting to be mined. The Eversons' meager financial resources deteriorated along with William's already fragile health. On January 20, 1889, William Everson died, leaving his wife and children to make their own way in the world.

Without her husband to handle the business aspects of her invention, Carrie gave up the hope of realizing any profit from her patent until she met Thomas Criley, a man with the imagination to see the value of her process and the financial resources to promote it.

Criley arranged to use an abandoned mill near Leadville for the early tests on the process. The first order of business was to construct machinery capable of performing the various functions according to Everson's instructions. With the help of

In the boom days of the Colorado gold strike, mining was a simple matter of digging a tunnel and bringing up the gold-laden ore. In the midst of such plenty, miners failed to see the value of Carrie Everson's oil flotation process.
(Courtesy Denver Public Library, Western History Department)

young John Everson, who was fascinated by his mother's work, Criley built an 800-gallon tank with revolving paddles and an adjustable partition. The test was simple and to the point. They filled the tank with water, poured in a mixture of oil and ore, then "stirred" it with the paddles. The partition separated the resulting mineral concentrate from the dross and wastewater. The results of these preliminary tests were not altogether successful, but they were promising.

Everson kept experimenting with different chemicals added to the oil bath and discovered that sulfuric acid, mixed in the proper ratios with cottonseed oil and water, had the desired effect. Despite a favorable article in the Denver *Daily News*, Colorado miners still saw no reason to bother with lower grade ores. Criley, who had the promotional ability that Everson lacked, decided that the process might be more attractive in Oregon. He journeyed to Baker County, where he experimented successfully with the sulfide ores that were mined at Silver Cliff.

Just when it looked as if the Oregon mining interests were ready to come aboard, Thomas Criley died unexpectedly and Everson found herself thrust into the hated role of business promoter. She did her best to pick up the negotiations that Criley had started, but to no avail. Without his skills as a manager, the deal fell through.

Carrie may have lacked a talent for self-promotion, but she was no stranger to hard work. Drawing upon the medical knowledge she had gained from her husband, she became a visiting nurse at the Denver Flower Mission. Some sources describe her work during this period as "obstetrical nursing," which indicates that she may have been a midwife, delivering babies in homes throughout the city. Regardless of her exact duties, she would have come into intimate contact with the kind of poverty she was trying to escape.

Between 1870 and 1887, the population of Denver had grown from 5,000 to 80,000; some were tuberculars who had come to seek a cure, and some were prospectors who had come to seek a fortune. Those who didn't find what they had sought ended up crowded together in the poorest neighborhoods of the city, struggling to survive.

A few months later, chemist Charles B. Hebron came on the scene, claiming to have experience in ore concentration. He worked with Everson on a variant of her basic idea. They jointly took out a new patent on this revised process in 1892. Many who have become interested in the history of Carrie Everson and her invention feel that she would have been better off sticking to her first formula. Hebron had ambition and an entrepreneur's sense of timing, but his chemical knowledge was not as extensive as was Everson's. Some of his changes proved to be less effective than her original method. Hebron convinced an investor known only as "Mr. Pischel" to finance testing in exchange for a share of the patent.

This time, the device for implementing the process was not a circular tank, but a rectangular "sluice box" with cleats spaced 2 feet apart along the bottom. The effect was like a sequence of speed bumps, which caused the matter to ripple and "wave" as it passed through the channel, carrying its load of ore, oil, and acid. By the time this mixture reached the end of the box, the mineral was separated from the waste materials and ready to be collected.

Though the tests succeeded, the partnership did not. Hebron and Pischel quarreled over the division of profits that didn't yet exist, and the entire enterprise fell apart. This time, Carrie Everson gave up hope of profiting by her invention, but she did not give up faith in the process itself. Years after the Hebron-Pischel partnership fell apart, John Everson would recall that his mother never stopped believing that the mining industry would one day see the value of flotation.

Carrie worked at the Denver Flower Mission until 1906, when she resigned to teach physiology and hygiene in the State Reformatory for Girls at Morrison, Colorado. Ironically, that was the first and only teaching experience this "schoolteacher from Denver" ever had. She worked at the school for three years, possibly living in staff quarters on the grounds. In 1909, she moved to the small California town of San Anselmo, where her son had been living for some years.

And so Carrie Everson disappeared from Colorado, not to be rediscovered until after her death. Even during the years of her quiet retirement, her story had another turn or two before coming to an end. After the last of Everson's patents had expired in 1912, the mining industry caught up with her thinking. When the supply of readily available metals and minerals dwindled, and boom towns threatened to turn into ghost towns, miners became vitally interested in tapping the resources of low-grade ores. When they began using a flotation process based on Everson's expired patent, the yields were large enough to satisfy even the most demanding investor.

This conspicuous success attracted the attention of a British company, Minerals Separation Limited, which claimed to own the oil flotation process and all patents relating to it. Minerals Separation filed suit against mining engineer James M. Hyde, claiming that he had infringed upon the company's patent by installing a flotation processing unit at a mine in Montana. The case threatened the entire American mining industry; if Minerals Separation won, nobody could use flotation mining without paying them a large royalty.

In February of 1914, the U.S. Circuit Court of Appeals heard the case in San Francisco. Hyde's attorneys wanted to call Carrie Everson as a witness. Her patent was taken out years before Minerals Separation filed an application or ran a single test. Her testimony could have cleared up the whole tangled mess, saving American mining interests a great deal of money in the bargain. Ironically, while Hyde's attorneys were searching for

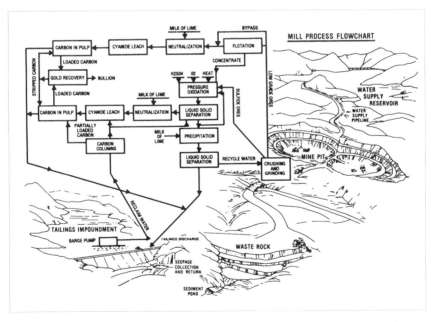

Flotation mining is still in use today. This flow chart shows the complex process used by Homestake Mining Company at its McLaughlin Mine in northern California.
(Courtesy Homestake Mining Company)

the elusive inventor, she lived just twenty miles away in San Anselmo.

Without Everson's testimony, James Hyde ultimately lost the case. In December 1916, the U.S. Supreme Court ruled in favor of Minerals Separation Limited, and American companies using flotation faced a huge increase in costs.

No one knows why Everson didn't come forward in 1914; even her son couldn't explain it. Perhaps she didn't want to get involved with the courts, or have anything to do with the process that had claimed so many years of her life. Perhaps she didn't hear about the case. Perhaps, after all those years, she simply didn't care.

Carrie Everson died on November 3, 1914, never having received a cent from the proceeds of her invention.

Chronology

August 27, 1842	Carrie Jane Billings born near Sharon, Massachusetts
1851	family moved to Springfield, Illinois
October 3, 1864	marries William Knight Everson
1878	Dr. Everson invests in mining venture Eversons move to Denver
early 1880s	Dr. Everson goes to Mexico Carrie begins her research in mineralogy
August 24,1886	receives patent on oil flotation process
January 20, 1889	Dr. Everson dies
1890–91	Carrie enters partnership with Criley Silver Cliff experiments Criley dies
1892	Carrie goes to work at Denver Flower Mission Carrie works on new process with Charles Hebron
1906	leaves mission to work at state school
1909	moves to California
1912	patents expire
November 3, 1914	dies in San Anselmo, California
July, 1915	Colorado Scientific Society search for Everson begins
January 15,1916	Carrie Everson honored posthumously in *Metallurgical and Chemical Engineering* magazine

Further Reading

Material on Everson is difficult to find, existing mostly in old magazine and newspaper articles. Two books that tell something about her life and work are:

Macdonald, Anne L. *Feminine Ingenuity: Women and Invention in America*. New York: Ballantine Books, Inc., 1992.
Vare, Ethlie Ann and Greg Ptacek. *Mothers of Invention*. New York: William Morrow and Co., 1988.

Books dealing with Colorado and gold rush history include:

Lee, Mabel Barbee. *Cripple Creek Days*. Lincoln, Nebr.: University of Nebraska Press, 1984. One woman's memories of life in Cripple Creek, Colorado, in 1892.
Robertson, Janet. *Magnificent Mountain Women*. Lincoln, Nebr.: University of Nebraska Press, 1990. An entertaining look at the lives of women in the Rockies during the gold rush.

Sara Josephine Baker, M.D. (1873–1945)

Sara Josephine Baker was not only an inventor, but also a pioneer in the field of public health. Many of the principles and practices she established in the impoverished tenement neighborhoods of New York City are still in use today.
(Courtesy Sophia Smith Collection, Smith College)

At the turn of the twentieth century, immigrant families crowded together in the tenements of New York City, scratching for a toehold in their adopted land. Hundreds of babies born into these harsh conditions died during their first fragile months of life. Hundreds more were blinded at birth by gonorrheal infections, sickened by tainted milk, or crippled by malnutrition.

Dr. Sara Josephine Baker was determined to change all that. Many of the afflictions that ran rampant through the tenements could be cured or prevented altogether: a drop of 1 percent silver nitrate solution in each eye immediately after birth prevented blindness from gonorrhea; pasteurization purified the milk supply; and dietary adjustments improved general health and resistance to disease. The problem was getting these measures to the people.

To accomplish that goal, Dr. Baker became a pioneer in public health, creating the first "bureau of child hygiene" in the country. She invented a dropper to administer measured dosages of silver nitrate and designed safe baby clothes after discovering that infants were being strangled to death by their ornate and impractical garments.

"A baby has the right to be born whole," Dr. Baker once said. Because of her efforts to protect that right, hundreds of babies who would have died survived to have children of their own; hundreds who would have been disabled enjoyed good health. In a very real sense, the public-supported child health program was as much her "invention" as the measured-dose dropper.

Sara Josephine Baker was born on November 15, 1873, in Poughkeepsie, New York, daughter of attorney O. D. M. (Orlando Daniel Mosher) Baker and Jenny Harwood Baker. Her father was self-educated, having left home as a boy to escape a stepmother he disliked. Her mother was a member of the first class to graduate from Vassar. The household was prosperous and happy, and Josephine, as Baker was called, and her sister Mary were well schooled in the domestic arts.

Looking back on those days, Josephine remembered hayrides and sing-alongs, dance cotillions, taffy pulls, and sneaking out of the house on the night the circus came to town. She and her brother and a neighborhood friend would spend the night watching roustabouts use elephants to set up the tent

> **❧ "I** was reared in a thoroughly conventional tradition and took to it happily. I understood that after I left school I would go to Vassar, and then, I supposed, I would get married and raise a family and that would be that."

by the weird-glowing light of kerosene torches. Until she was sixteen, Josephine Baker saw the world as "a unit with no gaps or turning points."

That was when her safe and tidy, seamless world fell apart. First, the sudden death of her beloved thirteen-year-old brother devastated the entire family. Three months later, her father died in a typhoid fever outbreak that swept the town. When his estate was settled, the family faced financial hardship for the first time in Josephine's life.

Her plan to attend Vassar went by the wayside. There was neither time nor money for a liberal arts education. One of the family would have to earn a living for all, and Josephine was elected. Doubtless, her mother expected her to become a teacher, a nurse, or perhaps a librarian, one of the occupations that was considered respectable for a young woman who was forced by circumstances to earn a living.

Instead, Josephine chose to attend the Women's Medical College of the New York Infirmary for Women and Children and train to become a doctor. Her mother and sister, along with a steady parade of relatives and friends, tried to discourage her. Medicine was no life for a young girl they said.

In meeting their objections, the future Dr. Baker showed the firm resolve that would serve her well later in life. She listened politely but never wavered from her objective. In 1894, she moved to New York City to begin her training. Four years later, she graduated second in a class of eighteen. Her distinguished record was marred by a single failure: she simply could not muster the interest to pass Dr. Annie Sturges Daniel's course in child development. Later in life, Dr. Baker would see a fine irony in her lack of interest in the field that was to become her life's work.

After graduation came internship at the New England Hospital for Women and Children in Boston. There, Dr. Baker got her first taste of working in the slums of a big city during a three-month stint in an outpatient clinic. It was a different world from any she had known, but to her own surprise, Dr. Baker was equal to the task. It stood her in good stead in 1901, when she was hired as a medical inspector for the New York City Department of Health at a salary of $30 per month. Her first assignment was to spend a summer working in the infamous "Hell's Kitchen," a place of poverty, sickness, and hopelessness. According to missionary William T. Elsing:

> An ordinary tenement-house contains five stories and a basement, four families usually occupying a floor. . . . In winter, just before the gas is lighted, dungeon darkness reigns. . . . More than once I have stumbled against a baby who was quietly sitting in the dark hall or on the stairs. In the old-style halls, there is no way of getting light and air. . . .

These early years with the Health Department were a time of learning and growing, not just for Dr. Baker, but for the entire staff. The field of public health was in its infancy then, the concept of preventive medicine only beginning to take shape. Dr. Baker helped give them form, and in the process found her own career.

Unlike conventional medicine, which focuses on treatment of individuals, public health focuses on whole communities. Preventing the spread of communicable diseases involves many strategies: sanitation, vaccination, some old-fashioned detective work, and a great deal of public education.

During this early work with hygiene and disease control, Dr. Baker observed the midwives who went into tenement apartments to deliver babies. Some were clean, knowledgeable, and cool in a crisis; others had no concept of sanitary procedures, nor were they capable of dealing with unexpected emergencies in the birthing process. Replacing these women with physicians was impossible; there simply weren't enough doctors to go around, and the poorest families couldn't afford them anyway.

Establishing standards for midwives would be more realistic, perhaps through a licensing requirement. In the process of working on the problem, Dr. Baker had her first glimmer of a more ambitious idea: a program to reduce infant mortality on a large scale. The idea stayed with her, nagging at the back of her mind while she worked on other projects.

In 1907, Dr. Baker won the official title of assistant to the commissioner of health. According to her, that was a high-sounding way of saying "trouble shooter." She did the things that didn't fit anybody else's job description. Often, these duties required her to be inventive and even a little outrageous.

For example, when she was assigned to organize mass smallpox vaccinations in the Bowery, she encountered immediate resistance. No matter how she reasoned, threatened, or begged, transients wouldn't come to the Health Department. Some were too drunk, some too suspicious, and some were just plain scared.

After much thought and frustration, Dr. Baker decided that if the people wouldn't come to the Health Department, then she would take the Health Department to them. She led a team on the rounds of Bowery "flop houses," where homeless men paid ten cents a night to sleep in threadbare blankets on a filthy floor.

Beginning at three or four in the morning, before even the earliest risers would be up and about, Dr. Baker and her team worked their way down the rows, inoculating each grumbling, half-wakened man before he had time to protest.

Not long after earning her promotion, Josephine Baker faced one of the most intriguing challenges of her career: apprehending the infamous "Typhoid Mary." Mary Mallon was a hard-working woman who prized her reputation as a fine cook. Unfortunately, she was also a typhoid carrier. Never stricken with the disease herself, Mary's body was what Dr. Baker called "a living culture of typhoid bacilli."

George A. Soper, a sanitary engineer in the Department of Health, discovered Mary when he was following a curious trail of typhoid outbreaks in private homes. He discovered that these families had one thing in common: each had employed a cook named Mary Mallon. In 1907, he located Mary working in a house on Park Avenue and asked for someone from the department to get specimens of her blood and urine.

Dr. Baker drew the assignment. Mary was polite enough until she learned the purpose of Dr. Baker's visit. Then she became steely eyed and grim, flatly refusing to allow any tests. That first meeting ended in a standoff, with Dr. Baker making a strategic retreat to consider her options. At the next meeting, Mary attacked Dr. Baker with a kitchen fork and had to be restrained in the ambulance that came to take Mary to the hospital laboratory. "I literally sat on her all the way," recalled Dr. Baker. "It was like being in a cage with an angry lion."

Typhoid Mary refused to believe that something called a "germ," which she couldn't even see, made her a hazard to anyone who ate her food. If she had agreed not to handle food and observed a few other restrictions, Mary Mallon could have gone free. But she was a cook, and she was not about to change.

Twice she was quarantined at a facility on North Brother Island in the East River, and twice she was released upon her solemn promise not to handle other people's food. Both times, she went back to earning her living in the only way she knew how: as a cook. Dr. Baker finally recommended that Mary be placed under lifetime quarantine on North Brother Island. She died there on November 11, 1938, at the age of seventy.

Bringing in Typhoid Mary secured Dr. Baker's place in one of history's most fascinating episodes. From her own viewpoint, the case was a living illustration of the power residing in public health officials. They could close a business, quarantine a home, imprison a disease carrier without due process of law— all in the name of the public good.

Only a few months after the Typhoid Mary incident, Dr. Baker was assigned to work with a privately financed research group that was investigating New York City's soaring death rate. What they found stunned the entire Health Departm... and became the last piece in a puzzle that Dr. Baker h...

> ❧ "The way to keep people from dying from disease, it struck me suddenly, was to keep them from falling ill. Healthy people didn't die. That sounds like a completely absurd and witless remark, but at that time it really was a startling idea."

putting together since she joined the department in 1901. The death rate was so high because of the thousands of babies and young children who died before they really got a chance to live. Through the summer months, 1,500 infants died every week, most of infectious diarrheal conditions that thrived in the muggy heat. These were preventable deaths.

With the backing of the health department, Dr. Baker asked for funds to conduct an experiment in preventive medicine. The idea of treating people before they got sick was a radical one at the time; the term "public health education" had not been invented.

For her experiment, Dr. Baker chose "a complicated, filthy, sunless and stifling nest of tenements on the lower east side." It had one of the highest infant mortality rates in the city. The program was simple and straightforward. With a staff of thirty public health nurses, the project reached every newborn in the neighborhood. The registrar of records supplied the names and addresses on a daily basis; the nurses did the visitations.

The things they taught these immigrant mothers seem obvious by today's standards. In 1908, they were revolutionary. They included breast-feeding (milk was still unpasteurized and therefore unsafe); adequate ventilation; frequent bathing; thin, nonbinding summer clothes; and a daily airing in the park. The nurses did regular followups to make sure mother and baby were doing well.

At the end of the summer, even Dr. Baker was stunned by ~ults of these simple measures: the experimental neigh- ~d 1,200 fewer deaths than the summer before. ~ town, the summer death rate of babies ever. On the basis of those outstanding ~nt created a new Division (soon to be

Sara Josephine Baker, M.D.

At the turn of the twentieth century, immigrants poured into the United States, seeking a better life for themselves and their families. Most of them lived in grim city tenements, where poverty and disease took their toll.
(Courtesy Ellis Island Immigration Museum)

"Bureau") of Child Hygiene, with S. Josephine Baker, M.D. as its chief. It was the first tax-supported agency devoted entirely to the health problems of infants and children.

Dr. Baker headed the agency until 1923; during her tenure she also became the first woman to earn a doctorate in public health (1917). As chief of the Division of Child Hygiene, she revolutionized public attitudes toward health education and preventive medicine. She established "Baby Health Stations," which dispensed pure milk and free childcare advice to the poor. She devised solutions to odd and unanticipated problems by using her considerable ingenuity, liberally spiced with good old-fashioned common sense.

For example, when her crusade for better ventilation in infants' sleeping quarters ran into European prejudices about night air and drafts, she wasted little time expounding the virtues of fresh air; instead, she convinced the mothers to open the windows and fill the gap with a board. That allowed some air to get in around the edges. Dr. Baker called it "a reasonable compromise" under the circumstances.

When she discovered that half the babies in the department's foundling hospital died before they were one year old, she set out to find the reason why. The hygiene was excellent, the food nutritious, the nurses well trained. Still the babies died. Her investigations uncovered another odd fact: babies brought up in the tenements by loving mothers had a better survival rate than those reared in wealthy homes by trained nurses.

Decades later, researchers would establish a link between infant mortality and lack of the cuddling, hugging, crooning behavior we call "mothering." Dr. Baker had only a hunch to go on, one she hardly believed herself. She decided to follow it anyway. Tenement mothers who had been raising their own babies with bureau guidance were paid $10 a month to become foster mothers to these neglected but immaculately clean infants. The result? Within four years, the overall death rate was cut in half, and the foster babies thrived.

Dr. Baker's willingness to look for achievable solutions, rather than ideal ones, was a key to her success. When she discovered that hundreds of eight-, nine-, or ten-year-old girls were the primary caregivers for their infant brothers and sisters, she realized that nothing the bureau could do would eliminate this practice. Therefore, it made sense to teach these girls the basics of infant care. The bureau's "Little Mothers League" was popular with the painfully young caregivers and excited interest in countries all over the world.

In a similar vein, it was impossible to arrange for every expectant mother to receive care from an obstetrician, so Dr. Baker went back to the old idea of training and licensing midwives. Women who wished to qualify for a license could attend classes for free. Some of the newer methods were a problem for these minimally trained workers.

For example, administering a 1% silver nitrate solution in each eye immediately after birth could eliminate the risk of congenital blindness due to gonorrheal infection. Unfortunately, most midwives carried it in a bottle with an unsterile dropper and no reliable way to measure the concentration of the solution. Some babies were injured by accidental overdosages, some blinded because the midwife skipped the uncertain treatment altogether.

Facing the problem with her customary practicality, Dr. Baker set out to design a foolproof system for packaging and administering the solution. The result was a little package with two beeswax capsules, each with enough solution for one eye. They were packed with sterile needles for puncturing the tips, thus turning the capsules into disposable medicine droppers.

Dr. Baker's next invention began with the need to do something about the elaborate and uncomfortable baby garments of the day: abdominal band, shirt, diaper, underpetticoat, and 3-foot-long dress. Getting a squirming infant into three sets of armholes, then turning him this way and that to do all the buttons, was a tedious and frustrating chore. Even worse, babies had actually been strangled by their own clothes.

The design that Dr. Baker devised was simple but ingenious: open-down-the-front garments with nonbinding armholes and neckbands. These new "safe baby clothes" worked so well that McCall Pattern Company made patterns for them, paying Dr. Baker a 1-cent royalty on each one sold. The Metropolitan Life Insurance Company bought 200,000 patterns for distribution to its policyholders.

Josephine Baker was not by nature a tinkerer who enjoyed inventing for invention's sake. She was a problem-solver with a knack for identifying needs and then creating solutions. By the time she retired in 1923, the infant mortality rate in New York City had dropped from 111 per thousand to 66 per thousand. That figure, far more than the devices she invented or the programs she created, stood as the proudest achievement of her career.

Dr. Baker never married or had children of her own. Her life was her work, and she was happy to have it that way. Sara Josephine Baker died of cancer on February 22, 1945, at the age of seventy-five.

LIBRARY
DEXTER SCHOOLS
DEXTER, NM 88230

Chronology

November 15, 1873	Sara Josephine Baker born in Poughkeepsie, New York
1894	enters Women's Medical College of the New York Infirmary for Women and Children
1898	earns M.D. degree, graduating second in a class of eighteen
1901	becomes medical inspector for the New York City Department of Health
1907	apprehends "Typhoid Mary"
1908	conducts experimental program of preventive medicine and education
August 1908	named head of the newly created Division (later Bureau) of Child Hygiene
1908–1910	sets up "Baby Health Stations" in the poor neighborhoods of New York develops foster mother program for foundling infants establishes "Little Mothers League" invents measured-dose eyedropper designs safe baby clothes
1917	becomes first woman to earn a doctorate in public health
1923	retires from the Bureau of Child Hygiene
February 22, 1945	dies of cancer at the age of seventy-five

Further Reading

Baker, S. Josephine, M.D. *Fighting for Life*. New York: The Macmillan Company, 1939. Dr. Baker's autobiography.

Duffy, John. *The Sanitarians: A History of American Public Health*. Urbana, Ill.: University of Illinois Press, 1990. Survey of Public Health in the United States, mentions S. J. Baker in the index.

Elsing, William T. "Life in New York Tenement-Houses: As Seen By a City Missionary." *Gaslight New York Revisited*. Secaucus, N.J.: Castle Books, 1989. Background on the tenement neighborhoods in the nineteenth and early twentieth century.

Kaufman, Martin and Stuart Galishoff, Todd L. Savitt, eds. *Dictionary of American Medical Biography*. Westport, Conn.: Greenwood Press, 1984. Brief listing on S. J. Baker.

Leavitt, Judith Walzer and Ronald L. Numbers. *Sickness & Health in America: Readings in the History of Medicine and Public Health*. 2nd ed., rev., Madison: University of Wisconsin Press, 1985. The social history of medicine in America; continues into the early twentieth century. Mentions S. J. Baker in the index.

James, Edward T., Janet Wilson James, and Paul S. Boyer, eds. *Notable American Women 1607–1950: A Biographical Dictionary*. Cambridge, Mass.: The Belknap Press of Harvard University Press, 1971. Brief but reasonably detailed section on S. J. Baker.

O'Hearn, Elizabeth Moot. *Profiles of Pioneer Women Scientists*. Washington, D.C.: Acropolis Books, 1985. Chapter on S. J. Baker.

Stanley, Autumn. *Mothers and Daughters of Invention: Notes for a Revised History of Technology*. Metuchen, N.J.: Scarecrow Press, 1993.

Vare, Ethlie and Greg Ptacek. *Mothers of Invention*. New York: William Morrow and Co., 1988. Section on S. J. Baker.

Madam C. J. Walker

Madam C. J. Walker not only invented the products she sold, but used her own image to merchandise them. The idea was to show that ordinary women with distinctly African-American features could be attractive, even glamorous, without imitating whites.
(Courtesy Madam C. J. Walker Collection, Indiana Historical Society Library)

*A*t the beginning of the twentieth century, even the most inventive and hard-working women faced obstacles to success, based strictly on their gender. African-American women had to contend with racial prejudice as well as gender stereotyping. To make a living, working-class black women either labored on sharecropper farms, worked as servants in wealthy homes, or took in laundry. At a time when unskilled white workers earned around $11 a week, their African-American female counterparts averaged $1.50.

Despite this prevailing poverty and lack of opportunity, Sarah Breedlove Walker invented a hair-care preparation and turned it into a thriving business. In the process, she became America's first African-American woman millionaire.

Like many inventors who go on to build successful companies, Madam Walker not only had a good product, she had an intuitive "feel" for the market. She began her business at a time when women of all races were eager to buy new products that made them look better, feel cleaner, and smell nicer. The field of cosmetology was about to come into its own, and Madam C. J. Walker was on the cutting edge of its growth.

Sarah Breedlove was born on December 23, 1867, in Delta, Louisiana, the youngest child of former slaves Owen and Minerva Breedlove. The Breedloves died of yellow fever when Sarah was six, leaving her in the care of a brother who soon went to Denver to find work and a sister who scratched out a living by taking in laundry. When other little girls were playing with dolls, Sarah was scrubbing sheets on a corrugated metal washboard.

When Sarah was eleven, her sister Louvenia married Willie Powell, a cruel, demanding man who took an instant dislike to his young sister-in-law. Sarah endured the situation for three years, then she married day laborer Moses (Jeff) McWilliams, largely to get away from Powell and have a home of her own. She was fourteen years old at the time. Daughter Lelia was born three years later, on June 6, 1885.

The baby was barely two years old when Moses McWilliams was killed in an accident. His young widow found herself alone in the world, with a child to support and no marketable skills except doing laundry. Sympathetic neighbors suggested she head upriver, to St. Louis. Wages were higher there, they said, and there was no shortage of jobs for anyone willing to work.

In 1888, Sara McWilliams packed up the baby and her few belongings and caught a riverboat to St. Louis, where she became a washerwoman. It was not an easy life. "Taking in laundry," as it was called, involved long hours of backbreaking labor. Gallons of water had to be heated and poured into a wooden or metal washtub; the laundry was then scrubbed against a corrugated washboard, rinsed, treated with blueing (a product to counteract yellowing and dinginess), starched, and ironed.

The St. Louis years weren't all poverty and drudgery. Because she worked hard and maintained high standards for her work, she soon had all the customers she could handle. Each week, she tried to put aside some of her earnings in a college fund for Lelia. Sometimes it meant going without things she needed, but she was determined to give her daughter the kind of start that she never had; education, she believed, was the key to that future.

McWilliams joined the St. Paul African Methodist Episcopal Church and became active in its missionary society, a community service group that gave everyone a chance to help. People who couldn't donate money could still give their time to help the poor, the sick, or the stranger trying to get a toehold in a new city. Being able to help others despite her own poverty gave Sarah McWilliams a deep sense of satisfaction.

In 1904, the missionary society went in a body to hear a speech by Margaret Washington, wife of the famous educator Booker T. Washington. She was a compelling speaker in her own right, and a woman of poise and elegance. McWilliams observed her every gesture—everything she said and did—and what she wore. Most of all, she noted how Mrs. Washington's immaculate personal appearance contributed to her image as a person of importance.

That example inspired Sarah McWilliams to do something about her own appearance, starting with her troublesome hair. It was dry and broken, so thin in places that the scalp showed through. There were products on the market that claimed to recondition damaged hair, but nothing that worked for McWilliams. When she had exhausted all available options, she decided to formulate her own treatment. Like many inventors, McWilliams started with a flash of enthusiasm that soon turned into dogged determination.

In her washtubs, she combined and recombined ingredients, seeking the right formula by a process of trial and error. This sort of "kitchen chemistry" was in vogue at the time. Just about everybody made some cleaning and grooming preparations at home, working with simple formulas and readily available ingredients.

Women regularly rinsed their hair in lemon juice or vinegar, to enhance the color and remove soap film. A popular shampoo recipe called for 1 well-beaten egg, 1 ounce of the herb rosemary, and 1 pint of hot water. One hair ointment used 2 tablespoons castor oil and 2 tablespoons lard, mixed together with a few drops of rosemary oil for fragrance. A treatment to add sheen to dry hair used comfrey, chamomile, clover, and ender flowers steeped in hot water.

Beyond these common preparations, McWilliams knew no chemistry, nor did she know anything about the structure of human hair. She just kept plugging away at the problem. To the day she died, Sara McWilliams Walker claimed that the formula came to her in a dream. A "big black man" appeared and told her what to mix up for her hair. Some of the ingredients came from Africa, but she sent for them without hesitation and prepared the formula exactly as the man had instructed. Such flashes of insight are not uncommon in the history of invention. After long hours of trial and error, breakthrough ideas may appear in a dream, or come out of nowhere at the most unexpected times.

With great enthusiasm and high expectations, McWilliams mixed the formula and tried it on her damaged hair. The results were better than she had dared to hope; her hair was shinier, easier to manage. For the first time in years, it began to look healthy.

From Wonderful Hair Grower, *Madam Walker expanded the line until it contained a wide variety of personal care products for the African-American woman.*
(Courtesy Madam C. J. Walker Collection, Indiana Historical Society Library)

She tried her discovery on friends and relatives with excellent results. She soon discovered that her pomade could also be used to loosen the naturally tight curl of African-American hair, so it could be arranged in the popular styles of the day. She never called her product a "hair straightener," though others used the term.

Many African-American women looked down on hair straightening, regarding it as an attempt to imitate whites. Others said it was a simple matter of fashion: black women straightened their hair to style it; white women curled theirs for the same reason.

The process of straightening hair with McWilliams' Wonderful Hair Grower was a forerunner of what modern cosmetologists know as a "hot comb press." The treatment involved brushing and washing the hair, coating it with pomade for body and "glossine" for shine, then stretching it out with heated metal combs.

When McWilliams could not find the type of comb she needed for this work, she designed one with wide-gapped teeth to lift and separate the dense curls of African-American hair. Over half a century later, her idea reappeared in the metal or plastic picks so popular for grooming African-American hair.

After refining her products and methods, McWilliams began planning a business strategy. To give her enterprise a proper launching, she decided to leave St. Louis for the untried territory of Denver, Colorado. The brother who moved there so long ago had recently died, leaving a widow and four daughters. She could get a job and help them financially; they could help her adjust to a new home.

She discussed her business plan with friend and confidant Charles Joseph (C. J.) Walker, a newspaperman by trade. Walker knew advertising and business practice better than anyone in McWilliams' circle of friends. He readily agreed that Denver would be a good choice.

As she had done as a twenty-year-old widow seeking a better life for herself and her child, Sarah McWilliams gathered up her possessions and headed for new territory. This time she went alone; the sacrifices she had made over the years had paid off. Lelia was away at college in Knoxville, Tennessee.

Sarah McWilliams arrived in Denver with $1.50 in her purse and took a job as a cook to keep herself going while she launched the business. Mixing formulas in the evenings and plowing all her profits back into materials and advertising, she went door-to-door in African-American neighborhoods, dressed in an immaculate white blouse and long black skirt, carrying her products in a distinctive black case.

Her own lustrous hair was the best possible advertisement for the three preparations she sold at that time: Wonderful Hair Grower, Glossine, and Vegetable Shampoo.

She also started a mail-order business, relying on magazine and newspaper advertisements to being in customers. In building this part of the business, she corresponded frequently with her friend C. J. Walker, seeking his advice about promotional ideas. They became so close that Walker pulled up stakes in St. Louis and came to Denver. Friendship quickly blossomed into something more, and the two were married on January 4, 1906.

To lend her products a certain dignity and sense of allure, Mrs. Sarah Breedlove McWilliams Walker became Madam C. J. Walker—a name that would one day become prominent in African-American communities all over the country.

In a year's time, the Madam C.J. Walker Manufacturing Company moved into a spacious building in Denver's industrial district. Not content to rest on her laurels, Madam Walker opened a second office in Pittsburgh, where a growing African-American population offered a ready market for the Walker Hair Care System.

Lelia, graduated from college and ready to make her own mark in the business world, joined her there. They opened Lelia College, to train African-American women as "hair culturists" who would not just sell Walker products, but actually style their customers' hair. Madam Walker remained in Pittsburgh for only two years, then her old urge to move on to new places and new challenges reasserted itself.

She left Lelia in charge of the school and moved on to Indianapolis, Indiana, where she established what was to become the company's national headquarters. The location suited her needs perfectly. Not only was Indianapolis centrally located in the great American heartland, it was a major hub for the transcontinental railroad. With easy access to shipping, the Madam C.J. Walker Manufacturing Company could become a truly nationwide operation.

Business success came at personal cost. The Walkers had been disagreeing about the company since Denver; C. J. wanted to keep it small, Sarah wanted to make it huge. She kept adding new products, opening new schools, hiring new agents. Matters came to a head in Indianapolis, as the new factory and national offices became an inescapable reminder of the differences that divided the couple. The Walkers divorced in 1912.

Alone again, Madam Walker threw herself into the business with renewed zeal. She was becoming confident and self-assured, able to stand up for herself when the occasion called for it. She even dared to take on no less a personage than Booker T. Washington, when he refused to let her speak at a convention of the National Negro Business League. Apparently, the great African-American educator didn't think too highly of female entrepreneurs, for he blocked every effort to get Madam Walker on the podium.

She took matters into her own hands. Between speakers, she stood up and spoke in a strong, sure voice, upbraiding Washington for ignoring her. That day, she won the respect of the man whose wife was indirectly responsible for the washtub experiments that launched a business.

Madam Walker's stunning success in business was partly due to her knack for finding good people to work with her. Among her successful hires was F. B. Ransom, the young lawyer who managed the business; Alice Kelly, one of the first women in the country to work as a factory foreman; and Marjorie Joyner, a training supervisor who would one day invent a new type of permanent-wave machine. All were gifted African Americans who needed a chance in the world.

With these capable people to handle operations, Madam Walker went back to her traveling ways. She established herself as an expert in beauty culture by touring the country, giving lecture-demonstrations of her products and methods in homes, churches, and women's clubs. To keep her image before the public, Madam Walker featured her own picture on product labels, a practice that soon made her one of the most recognizable African Americans in the nation.

❧ "I am a woman who came from the cotton fields of the South. I was promoted from there to the washtub. Then I was promoted to the cook kitchen, and from there I *promoted myself* into the business of manufacturing hair goods and preparations. I have built my own factory on my own ground."

For regular sales and service, she relied upon her Walker Agents and the sort of door-to-door marketing that would later be used to great success by companies such as Avon and Mary Kay. Madam Walker's standards for agents were strict—everything about them had to be starched and pressed and spotless. Reaching back to her own beginnings in the world of business, Madam Walker devised the perfect uniform: immaculate white blouse, long black skirt, and distinctive black case. Walker training manuals often contained homey advice about customer relations: "Keep your teeth clean in order that the breath might be sweet. Five cents worth of mints will last a week. Put one in the mouth before beginning a customer. If her breath is offensive, offer her one."

These young women became a familiar sight in African-American neighborhoods. They not only carried samples, but the necessary supplies and equipment for dressing hair in the customer's own home. The company employed nearly 3,000 young women, giving them steady work at decent pay, and pride in themselves and the products they represented.

Every agent signed an employment contract, promising to use only Walker products and methods and to follow certain rules of hygiene. Those rules were years ahead of their time, setting standards in an industry that was not yet governed by legal codes. There were no government agencies to oversee the training and licensing of cosmetologists, no consumer "watchdogs" to protect the public from unscrupulous practices and worthless products.

Much of American business still operated on the ancient concept of *caveat emptor* ("let the buyer beware"); Madam Walker refused to sacrifice principle for profit. Customers soon learned that they could depend on Walker products and Walker people. The result was repeat business and a groundswell of word-of-mouth advertising as satisfied customers recommended Walker to their friends and relatives. The company became one of the most successful in the country; Madam Walker herself became a millionaire.

In 1913, at the urging of her daughter, Madam Walker moved to New York to extend her operations into the fabled African-American "city" called Harlem. Lelia, who had divorced her husband and added an "A'" in front of her given name, wanted to try her luck in the city. Madam Walker bought two houses on West 136th Street and remodeled them for a school and a beauty parlor, with living quarters for herself and A'Lelia on the upper floors. Company headquarters remained in Indianapolis.

Madam Walker was rich by this time, but she never forgot what it was like to be poor and disadvantaged. Harking back to her missionary society days in St. Louis, she worked with many charitable organizations and social action groups, giving her time and money to make life better for others. In 1913, she started a program to get company employees involved with worthy causes, organizing them into "Walker Clubs" and offering cash prizes to the clubs that did the most community service work.

There was a mood of activism in the land as reform-minded citizens crusaded for everything from labor unions to public health projects and votes for women. In African-American communities, this activism took on a special urgency as a generation that was less than fifty years removed from slavery sought its rightful place in society.

Leaders emerged to stand against bigotry and discrimination, among them gifted people such as W. E. B. DuBois, founder of the National Association for the Advancement of Colored People (NAACP), and Ida Wells-Barnett, who spoke out against the antiblack riots that swept the country between 1900 and 1914. Madam Walker's friend Charlotte Hawkings Brown established a private academy for African Americans who had been barred from white public high schools.

Madam Walker helped Brown start the Palmer Memorial Institute, gave thousands of dollars to the NAACP, and established scholarships for young women at the famed Tuskeegee Institute. She also helped the cause of African-American

The contrast of slave cabin and mansion became part of Madam Walker's legend. Villa Lewaro was a huge extravagance, but it gave work to dozens of African Americans, including architect Vertner Tandy.
(Courtesy Madam C. J. Walker Collection, Indiana Historical Society Library)

advancement by hiring black workers, patronizing black businesses, and encouraging the work of black artists and writers.

When she decided to build a luxurious home in upstate New York, she commissioned black architect Vertner Tandy to design it. He created a lavish, thirty-room mansion on the banks of the Hudson River. Madam Walker and A'Lelia took possession in June of 1918. The honor of naming the estate fell to famed opera singer Enrico Caruso, who suggested "Villa Lewaro," after the first syllables of A' Lelia Walker Robinson's married name.

Madame Walker was by this time in poor health, with soaring blood pressure and failing kidneys. Her doctor ordered her to slow down; a lifetime's experience made that next to impossible. There was always one more African-American group needing inspiration, one more worthy charity needing support.

During a visit to St. Louis in April of 1919, Madam Walker collapsed and was rushed to the hospital. When she felt well enough to be moved, friends took her home to Villa Lewaro, where she died of kidney disease on May 25, 1919, less than a year after moving into her mansion on the Hudson.

Thousands of people interrupted their busy lives to honor her memory and to praise her as inventor, business leader, and generous benefactor of worthy causes. That generosity continued even after death, in the thousands of dollars Madam Walker willed to favorite organizations, and in the hope she symbolized for African Americans struggling to make their way in an often hostile world.

Shortly after Madam Walker's death, company employees wrote a tribute to her memory:

The least we can say of her is that she was absolutely just and equitable in here dealings with us. We hereby testify that she did not gain her wealth by overworking or underpaying her employees. . . . In her establishment no employee was ill at ease when the employer appeared. . . . She was devoted to her helpers and so were they to her.

Chronology

December 23, 1867	Sarah Breedlove born in Delta, Louisiana
1884	marries Jeff McWilliams
1888	moves to St. Louis after McWilliams dies, takes work as washerwoman
1905	discovers her hair-care method moves to Denver, Colorado
January 4, 1906	marries newspaperman Charles J. Walker
1907	establishes offices in Denver
1908	opens additional plant in Pittsburgh
1910	moves plant to Indianapolis, Indiana
1913	organizes community service projects
1917	builds Villa Lewaro in upstate New York
May 25, 1919	dies at Villa Lewaro, of kidney disease

Further Reading

Bundles, A'Lelia Perry. *Madam C. J. Walker*. New York: Chelsea House Publishers, 1991. Young people's biography of Madam Walker, written by her great-great-granddaughter.

Colman, Penny. *Madam C. J. Walker*. Brookfield, Conn.: The Millbrook Press, 1994. Juvenile biography of Madam Walker.

Smith, Jessie Carney. *Notable Black American Women*. Detroit, Mich.: Gale Research, 1992. Fairly complete listing on Madam Walker.

Ida Rosenthal
1886–1973

Ida and William Rosenthal in 1912.
(Courtesy The Maidenform Museum, New York City)

*I*n the world of fashion, last season's styles are as out-of-date as yesterday's newspaper. The top designers live in endless pursuit of innovative styles, fresh colors, and contemporary fabrics. To create something that endures through these endless changes is quite an accomplishment. Ida Rosenthal, her husband, and her business partner did exactly that when they created the Maiden Form brassiere in the early 1920s.

The design conformed to the human body rather than the temporary dictates of fashion, an idea that seemed bold at the time. In the twenties, women wore tight bandeaux to flatten their chests for the skinny, skimpy "flapper" dresses everybody longed to wear. Before that, they had laced themselves into corsets so tight some wearers actually died of asphyxiation. Rosenthal's invention changed the shape of the American woman and opened new possibilities for the entire fashion industry.

Ida Kaganovich was born on January 9, 1886, in the little town of Rakov, Russia. The eldest of seven children born to Abraham and Sarah Kaganovich, Ida possessed an independent spirit and a bright, inquiring mind. Her father was a scribe from a family of scholars; her mother operated a general store. From them, young Ida acquired a love of learning, a knack for business, and a determination to do something with her life.

In Russia of the 1880s, the options open to girls were limited; mostly, they learned to be homemakers. A young woman's future didn't depend upon her own abilities and training, but upon the kind of man she married. Sarah Kaganovich wanted more for her daughters, so she convinced a local dressmaker to take Ida and her sister Ethel as apprentices.

After completing the training, Ida went to Warsaw to work and to attend classes at the gymnasium (high school). She met people with new and interesting ideas—Socialists, who wanted a society based on peace and sharing rather than war and competition. By the time Ida returned to Rakov, she had become hopelessly radical by local standards.

Through her involvement with the revolutionary movement, she met and fell in love with William Rosenthal. The two of them made a formidable team as they attempted to rouse public sentiment against the absolute power of the czar. Ida came

Ida Rosenthal and Enid Bissett outside their shop on West 57th Street.
(Courtesy The Maidenform Museum, New York City)

close to landing in jail when she made a fiery speech calling for the overthrow of the czarist regime. The chief of police warned Sarah Kaganovich that Ida's activism could land her in jail.

In 1905, William was conscripted into the army. Rather than serve a government he opposed, he fled to America. Ida followed some months later. The usual pattern for new immigrants was to settle in the squalid tenements of a large city and work in the nearest factory. It was a hand-to-mouth existence with no security and precious little comfort. Ida Kaganovich refused to live that way. With unbounded energy and her usual determination, she bought a sewing machine on time payments and set out to turn herself into the best dressmaker in Hoboken, New Jersey.

Though she was determined to make the business a success, she didn't intend to sacrifice her personal life in order to do it. In 1906, she married William, and a year later their son Lewis was born. With the additional responsibility of a child, the Rosenthals worked harder than ever. By 1912, Ida had a loyal clientele, six employees, and earned $6.50 to $7.50 per dress. The business continued to prosper, and the family continued to grow. Daughter Beatrice was born in 1916.

Two years later, the Rosenthals moved to 611 West 141st Street in Manhattan, where Ida set up a new shop. When she made some dresses for the director of her daughter's nursery school, she unknowingly set off a chain of events that would change the focus of her life.

Enid Bissett, owner of a dress boutique on New York's fashionable West 57th Street, saw the nursery school director wearing Rosenthal's dresses and was impressed by the deft interpretations of the current styles. She promptly hired the young seamstress as the dressmaker for Enid Frocks.

For a time, Rosenthal kept her own clients, but as Enid Frocks grew, the workload became daunting, even for a woman of her energy and skill. In 1921, Bissett offered her a partnership.

After considering the risks and the possible rewards, Rosenthal accepted Bissett's offer, investing $4,000—almost her entire life savings—to become an equal partner in the business.

> 💐 "Nature made woman with a bosom, so nature thought it was important. Why argue with nature? . . . A sister shouldn't look like a brother."

Enid Frocks specialized in high-quality, individualized fashions that ranged in price from $125 to $300 each: a staggering sum to pay for a dress in the early twenties. The partners kept a steady clientele by putting customer satisfaction ahead of the quick sale, and quality ahead of quantity.

Rosenthal and Bissett disliked the figure-flattening bandeaux that had come into fashion. They gave an artificial, boyish line to the figure, making precise fittings all but impossible. The most carefully constructed garment looked out of kilter when worn over the bandeaux. The partners began experimenting with a new kind of undergarment, one that would support the breasts and enhance the natural curves of the female form. They devised a garment with two cups, separated by a piece of elastic.

William Rosenthal, who had a flair for design, worked out the practical problems of construction, using existing techniques and equipment. The result was the first Maiden Form brassiere, which Ida and Enid sewed into their dresses to ensure a good fit.

They didn't think of the commercial potential of brassieres until clients began asking to buy them separately. Rosenthal coined the name "Maiden Form" to distinguish her design from the flat "boyish form" of the bandeaux. The first Maiden Form brassieres sold for $1 each, and were definitely a sideline to the dress business.

By 1925, the "sideline" had become the centerpiece of a growing business. Rosenthal and Bissett gave up the dress business altogether to manufacture and market the Maiden Form (later Maidenform) brassiere. The company opened a large manufacturing center in Bayonne, New Jersey, and hired dozens of sewing machine operators to make brassieres.

Rosenthal soon realized that traditional dressmaking methods would never keep up with demand. To mass-produce brassieres, the manufacturing facility needed to work more like a factory than a custom dress shop. A section-work process was the answer. She divided brassiere construction into separate tasks and set up a kind of assembly line. Instead of making a whole garment, each worker did a specific task, then passed the garment-in-progress down the line. This method is still used today in the intimate apparel industry.

By 1930, Enid Bissett had retired from active participation in the business, leaving its operation to the Rosenthals. As they had during their rebel days in czarist Russia, Ida and William made a formidable team. He served as president and chief designer; she headed sales, finance, and public relations.

Ida's keen business sense and vivacious personality made her an ideal company representative. To those who knew her, she

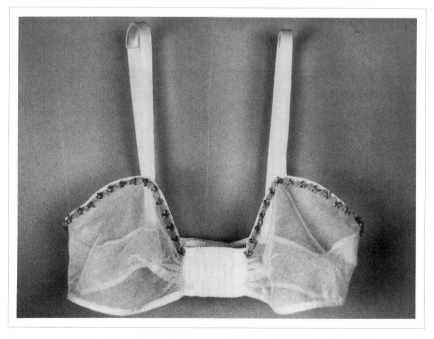

The 1922 Maiden Form brassiere was a deceptively simple design that caught on quickly because it improved the look and fit of women's clothing.
(Courtesy The Maidenform Museum, New York)

This 1927 advertisement prefigured the memorable campaigns that would begin with the famous "Maidenform dreams" series.
(Courtesy The Maidenform Museum, New York City)

became something of a legend in her own time. She was the crusader who got out of Russia one step ahead of the czarist police, the immigrant who made good, and the inventor who transformed the world of fashion. As dedicated as Rosenthal was to the business, she never let herself become obsessed with it to the exclusion of everything else. She loved to travel, attend the theater, and spend time with her family. Both she and

William were active in supporting many worthwhile community programs.

They endowed a Boy Scout camp in memory of their son, Lewis, who died in 1930, while attending law school at Columbia University. Over the years, Camp Lewis has provided growth experiences for hundreds of young people in the Bayonne area. The Rosenthals also established a foundation to fund arts, education, and social service programs all over the country. To their way of thinking, giving was as much a part of good business practice as was making profits.

Unlike many entrepreneurs who start with an idea and build it into a business, Ida Rosenthal didn't grasp at short-term solutions for long-term situations. She planned ahead, with three goals in mind: to produce a quality product, make Maiden Form one of the best-known brand names in the world, and develop a corporate structure that would survive into the next generation and beyond. Over an active career that lasted into the mid-1960s, she accomplished all these objectives.

When World War II caused shortages in civilian manufacturing, Rosenthal convinced the War Department that women working in defense industries needed brassieres for proper support and comfort. Throughout the war, Maiden Form received priority shipments of fabric and supplies to make brassieres for women involved in the war effort.

While normal production was cut back, many companies couldn't see the point of advertising products no one could buy, so they slashed promotional budgets and settled back to wait out the war. Ida Rosenthal considered that shortsighted. She advertised extensively, to keep the Maiden Form name before the public. As a result, sales figures soared as soon as normal production resumed.

Merchandising changed after the war, particularly with products aimed at women. World War II had been the time of "Rosie the Riveter." The mythic Rosie became the embodiment of all the women who did what was considered a man's job, while the men were away at war. They built ships, served as

❦ "So numerous are the Rosenthals in the company that Maidenform employees differentiate them by first name or initial. Thus Moses is Mr. Moe, Ellis is Mr. Ellis, and the dominant couple, Mr. and Mrs. R. But there is this difference between Mrs. R. and the others; they may know design, or production, or standard, but Mrs. R. knows everything."

brakemen on trains, plowed farmland, drove trucks, and even played professional baseball.

After the war, when the men came home, thousands of Rosies got their notice: the emergency's over and thanks a lot, but now go back to the kitchen. Most did go back, but found it difficult to adjust to their former lives. As housewives, they lost the independence and sense of adventure that had sustained them through the war.

Ida Rosenthal had always insisted that Maiden Form stay in tune with the times, and in touch with the lives of its customers. As a girl in Russia, she had experienced the limitations placed on women; as an entrepreneur in America, she had defied those limits to make a role for herself in the world of work. She understood the predicament of the ex-Rosies; all they could do was dream.

This sensitivity to the unspoken yearnings of the women who bought and used Maiden Form products produced one of the most memorable advertising programs in history: the famous dream campaign, which lasted for more than twenty years.

It began in August of 1949, with "I dreamed I went shopping in my Maiden Form bra." *Maiden Form* became *Maidenform* as approximately 170 dream ads showed women as adventurous achievers in lush and exotic settings. Top designers of the day created fanciful costumes that shared one striking detail— instead of a blouse or a dress bodice, each model wore only a Maidenform bra. The effect was whimsical and fun, done with a dash of bravado, a wink, and a smile. A single line of copy linked the series together: "I dreamed I . . . in my Maidenform bra."

Everyone waited to see how each new Maidenform dream would fill in the blanks. In magazines all over the country, women "went to blazes," "painted the town red," and "took the bull by the horns" in their Maidenform bras.

While these fantasy adventures delighted the public, the woman who started it all lived a real-life adventure of her own. In 1963, Ida Rosenthal returned to Russia as the only woman member of an American trade delegation. The girl who fled repression with nothing but determination and her hard-won skills as a dressmaker returned as an inventor, a community benefactor, and a successful corporate executive.

William wasn't alive to share this moment. He had died in 1958, leaving Ida to carry on the business. For a while, she served as president; then she decided it was time for the second generation to begin shaping the company. Daughter Beatrice and her husband, Dr. Joseph A. Coleman, were ready for the challenge; Ida felt sure that they would carry on the tradition in fine style.

Beatrice had joined Maiden Form in 1938, right after her graduation from Barnard College. Husband Joseph came aboard after the war and quickly showed himself to be a perceptive administrator. In 1959, he succeeded Ida as president of the company. She became chairman of the board.

Ida Rosenthal never retired; as she liked to say, she didn't have time for that. In 1966, at the age of eighty and away from home on yet another business trip, she suffered a stroke that left her incapacitated until her death in 1973. If a single word could describe the life and work of this remarkable woman, that word would be "adaptability."

❦ "The Maiden Form brand name was prized by women around the world. A 1942 *Vogue* article, written by a woman in South India preparing to flee before the invading Japanese force, describes how she sent to her home for the few items she wanted. Among them were 'the last two Maiden Form bras I had from America and which I had been saving.'"

As an immigrant, she adapted herself to a new country, a new language, and a new way of life. As an inventor, she adapted a simple bandeau into a shape that suited her customers' needs; and as a business executive, she adapted and readapted her merchandising strategies to the demands of a changing market.

Her spirit, if not her active participation, was there when daughter Beatrice scrapped the dream campaign to keep the company in tune with changing realities. Beatrice Rosenthal Coleman, who took over the presidency after the death of her husband in 1968, realized that the expectations and ambitions of American women were different from what they had been in 1949. Fantasies weren't enough anymore; women wanted real achievement. They reentered the work force in record numbers, many choosing occupations that once belonged exclusively to men.

Into the late 1970s and early 1980s, Maidenform's ads portrayed women in active or professional roles. The imagination and humor remained intact, as did the Maidenform bra. The caption? "The Maidenform Woman: You Never Know Where She'll Turn Up."

The same could have been said for Ida Rosenthal, who transformed a dressmaker's improvised solution to a fitting problem into a multimillion-dollar corporation.

Chronology

January 9, 1886	Ida Kaganovich born in Rakov, Russia
1905	emigrates to the United States
1906	marries William Rosenthal
1907	son Lewis born
1912	employs six workers in her dressmaking business
1916	daughter Beatrice born
1918	moves to Manhattan, shop on West 141st St.
1921	joins Enid Bissett in custom dress boutique
1922	creates the first Maiden Form bra registers the trade name, "Maiden Form"
1925	gives up dress business to make brassieres sets up assembly line form of construction
1930	Enid Bissett retires from active participation in company
1938	donates land for Camp Lewis, Boy Scout Camp
1941	institutes wartime production schedules
1949	dream campaign begins
1953	establishes the Ida and William Rosenthal Foundation
1958	William Rosenthal dies
1963	returns to Russia as member of U.S. Trade Delegation
1966	suffers incapacitating stroke
March 28, 1973	dies in New York City

Further Reading

Magill, Frank N., ed. *Great Lives from History: American Women*. Pasadena, Calif.: Salem Press, 1995. Fairly extensive biography of Rosenthal.

Moog, Carol. *Are They Selling Her Lips? Advertising and Identity* New York: William Morrow and Co., 1990. Chapter on Maidenform's groundbreaking advertising campaigns.

Morris, Michele. "The Mother Figure of Maidenform." *Working Woman*. April, 1987. Article on Beatrice Coleman, citing Ida Rosenthal's strong example and influence on her daughter's success.

Sicherman, Barbara, and Carol Hurd Green, with Ilene Kantrov and Harriette Walker, eds. *Notable American Women: The Modern Period*. Cambridge, Mass.: The Belknap Press of Harvard University Press, 1980. Section on Rosenthal.

Vare, Ethlie Ann and Greg Ptacek. *Mothers of Invention*. New York: William Morrow and Co., 1988. Section on Ida Rosenthal.

Katharine Blodgett
(1898–1979)

"Katie" Blodgett at work in her laboratory at General Electric's research facility in Schenectady, New York
(Courtesy Hall of History Foundation, Schnectady, New York)

*I*n science, breakthroughs often happen because somebody looks at the familiar in a fresh new way, often producing dramatic results from seemingly inconsequential observations. For example, any eight-year-old with a jar of "bubble stuff" and a plastic blower knows that soap bubbles change color as they change size. Dr. Katharine Blodgett observed this familiar phenomenon and realized that the change was related to the thickness of the soap film. By exploring that discovery, she developed a color gauge that could measure films so thin they could not even be seen under a microscope.

In a long and varied career, she also invented a gas mask that saved lives during World War I, and a smokescreen that saved them during World War II. Her best-known discovery is the "invisible glass" that makes everything from periscopes to picture frames more efficient and easier on the eyes.

Dr. Blodgett is the perfect example of how a good theoretician can bridge the gaps between scientific disciplines, and between applied technology and pure research. She worked in that intellectual borderland where the disciplines of physics and chemistry overlap—sometimes as a scientist, pursuing knowledge for its own sake, sometimes as an inventor, transforming theory into applied technology.

Katharine Burr Blodgett was born January 10, 1898, in Schenectady, New York, a few weeks after her father's death. George Bedington Blodgett was a patent attorney for the General Electric Company who apparently left his family in a comfortable financial situation. Katie, as everyone called her, attended the finest private schools, where girls received the same quality of academic education as boys.

She demonstrated a talent for mathematics early in life. Before she knew the alphabet she could recite the multiplication tables and a considerable portion of what she called "the gosintas"—two goes into four, three goes into six, and so forth. Rather than discourage this interest as "unfeminine," Katharine Blodgett taught her namesake to be proud of her abilities.

Unlike the typical image of the aloof and socially inept scholar, Katie had a high sense of fun and the ability to make friends easily. At 5 feet, 2 inches tall, with a trim figure and an upturned nose, she possessed the appearance of someone people might describe as "cute"—at least until they saw her restless, creative intellect go into action.

Katharine Blodgett

Katie graduated from high school at the age of fifteen and won a scholarship to Bryn Mawr College, where an inspiring physics professor fired her interest in science. During Christmas vacation of her senior year, she made a sentimental journey to Schenectady, the town where she had been born, and where the father she never knew had died.

Partly from curiosity and partly from a desire to see the place where he used to work, she visited the General Electric research laboratories. A chemist named Irving Langmuir showed her around. Langmuir recognized ability when he saw it; and he saw it in Katharine Blodgett. Before the tour was over, he advised her to continue her scientific education.

Blodgett followed his advice. In 1917, she graduated from Bryn Mawr and went straight to the University of Chicago, where she earned her master's degree in chemistry with a timely thesis on the absorption of gasses by carbon. This research proved invaluable for designing effective gas masks during World War I.

With World War I raging through Europe, that topic wasn't just scientifically interesting; it had become a matter of life and death. For the first time in history, poisonous gasses were being used as weapons of war. The military drew upon Blodgett's research to make improvements in gas mask design. Many a veteran of that brutal war may have owed his survival to a brilliant graduate student who faced an uncertain professional future.

In 1918, "young ladies" became wives and mothers, not research scientists. Katharine Blodgett was luckier than most women who chose to defy the feminine stereotype. Her thesis had already yielded practical benefits, and she had contacts at the General Electric laboratory in Schenectady, people who had known and respected her late father. Even the inevitable personnel shortage of wartime was on her side. With so many men overseas, American businesses were more open to hiring qualified women.

As soon as she had her master's degree in hand, Katie Blodgett packed her bags and headed for Schenectady. General

> ❦ "A woman who wants to do something in science must have three things besides formal training—patience, persistence and a knack at solving problems, or at least the desire to try to solve them. A girl who is not interested in the little problems of everyday life will not find it easy to learn to solve the problems of work in a laboratory."

Electric hired her on the spot, making her the first female research scientist in company history.

Blodgett settled into her new environment and soon made herself a valuable part of the research team. Between 1918 and 1924, she collaborated with Irving Langmuir on half a dozen major papers. It was Langmuir who suggested that she pursue a doctorate at Cambridge University in England.

The doctoral program was all Blodgett had hoped for, but the living conditions were less than ideal. Cambridge was a place of damp, bone-chilling cold and unheated classrooms. For two years, she lived in layered woolen clothing and pursued her studies with single-minded dedication. In 1926, she added yet another first to her growing resume, becoming the first woman in history to receive a Ph.D. in physics from Cambridge.

Back home in Schenectady, she slipped into her familiar routine. Her first assignment was to work with Dr. Langmuir on a study of tungsten filaments in electric lamps. Part of that apparently routine research would change the direction of Dr. Blodgett's entire career. She and Langmuir had studied the formation of hydrogen and oxygen films on tungsten, noting how these films were affected by varying degrees of heat. The whole subject of *monomolecular layers* (surface films no thicker than a single molecule) fascinated Dr. Blodgett. These ultra-thin layers seemed to be a law unto themselves, exhibiting peculiar two-dimensional qualities. As coverings on living membranes, they are important in the action of enzymes and other biological substances. Understanding them could lead to measuring the molecular sizes of viruses and toxins, a significant breakthrough for biologists seeking the causes and cures of various diseases. No one had even begun to explore their technological potential.

Katharine Blodgett wanted to try. As her supervisor, Dr. Langmuir was only too happy to give her the go ahead. For several months, Blodgett worked relentlessly without turning up anything new. One December afternoon in 1933, when she was tired, discouraged, and more than ready to call it a day, she pushed herself to try one more experiment. She floated a film of stearic acid on top of ordinary tap water and lowered a metal plate into it. To her surprise, the acid film moved toward the plate, coating it evenly as it went down into the water.

She expected the acid to refloat on top of the water when she pulled the plate back up. Instead, another layer of film attached itself on top of the first. Together, they were about 2/10,000,000 of an inch in thickness. Blodgett soon succeeded in building up 200 separate layers of oil film on a piece of ordinary window glass. Then she noticed something interesting; as thickness changed, so did color. The relationship never varied; x number of layers always produced one certain color.

Dr. Blodgett realized that she had found a method for making precise measurements of any transparent or semitransparent substance. The most sensitive instruments available were accurate to only a few thousandths of an inch; Blodgett's gauge could give precise measurements down to less than one millionth of an inch. A glass "ruler" showed the progression of colors corresponding to different thicknesses. Measurement was a simple matter of matching colors.

Over the years, Dr. Blodgett's gauge has proved useful in many different scientific disciplines. Metallurgists have used it to examine oxide coatings on steel, biochemists to measure the swelling of tiny blood corpuscles, and biologists to study the action of antigens upon antibodies.

The color gauge was an impressive achievement, but Katharine Blodgett wasn't a person to rest on her laurels. Now thoroughly committed to her ongoing research in surface chemistry, she hardly broke stride before undertaking another series of experiments, this time to explore the optical properties of monomolecular layers.

Though she was patient, thorough, perhaps even obsessive about her work, Dr. Blodgett also valued a balanced life. She was an actress with Schenectady's little theater group, a dedicated worker for civic and charitable organizations, and a thoughtful friend to coworkers and neighbors. She also had a most unscientific predilection for writing corny verses and parodies of old songs. A coworker's challenge to find a rhyme for "formaldehyde polyvinyl" resulted in this gem:

That formaldehyde polyvinyl—
If you eat it, you're certain to dine ill.
One night at a party,
When the guests all ate hearty,
By actual count it made nine ill.

She needed this sense of fun as a counterbalance to the intensity of her research as she got deeper into the study of monomolecular layers. Dr. Langmuir joined her in this phase of the research as together they investigated the properties of these invisible layers.

At one point in the research, Dr. Blodgett succeeded in building up 3,000 separate monomolecular layers. As she built up the layers and examined their interactions, she functioned as a chemist. When she studied their light refracting properties, she stepped over into the realm of physics. Moving back and forth between the two disciplines, Dr. Blodgett discovered that exactly 44 monomolecular layers of liquid soap prevented the glass from reflecting light.

When light passes through untreated glass, part of it strikes the surface and bounces back, creating what we call glare. Not only does this reflected glare interfere with our vision, it represents an overall loss in lighting efficiency. Nonreflective glass allows 99% of the light that strikes it to pass through. In the case of optical devices such as camera lenses and submarine telescopes, that high level of efficiency can be very important indeed.

On December 27, 1938, the General Electric laboratory announced Dr. Blodgett's invention to the press. At that point, the nonreflective film was not yet a workable technology. The coating process worked efficiently enough, but the coatings themselves were far too soft to be of practical value. General Electric never tried to commercialize the process. Instead, the company made the experimental data freely available to everyone.

The announcement of what the press insisted on calling "invisible glass" created quite a sensation. Scientists welcomed the news because they felt certain that technology would find a way around the permanency problem. A durable film could increase the efficiency of lens systems in periscopes, cameras, and other optical instruments. The public welcomed it with visions of nonglare shop windows, and auto windshields that didn't blind oncoming drivers with reflected light.

Though Dr. Blodgett continued her work with surface chemistry, she basically left the development of a durable nonreflective film to others. In December of 1941, the United States' entry into World War II reshaped the priorities of the entire American scientific community. Dr. Blodgett put all other research questions aside to concentrate on military projects. Her most outstanding work during this period was a new type of smoke generating device. The army was using simple "smudge pots," similar to those used in citrus groves to protect the fruit from overnight freezes.

These small devices were completely inadequate for the army's purpose, which was to lay down thick, billowing smoke to hide Allied troops from enemy attack. They needed a dense smoke that would not dissipate too quickly, and a machine capable of generating it. Dr. Blodgett got to work, and soon developed exactly what the army wanted: a machine that operated on two quarts of oil and that could spread vast quantities of long-lasting smoke over several acres. The smokescreen saved many lives by providing cover for troops who operated in

Katharine Blodgett's highly efficient smokescreen device saved hundreds of lives during World War II. Here, the men of the 84th Chemical Smoke Generating Company lay down a screen to cover army engineers as they build a pontoon bridge across the Moselle River (March 1945).
(Courtesy U.S. Army Military History Institute)

open spaces where they would have otherwise been vulnerable to surprise attack.

Over her distinguished career, Dr. Blodgett earned many honors and awards, including the American Association of University Women achievement award in 1945, and the coveted Garvan medal of the American Chemical Society in 1951. Also in 1951, the mayor of Schenectady declared June 13 as "Katharine Blodgett Day," honoring Dr. Blodgett as a brilliant scientist and concerned citizen:

> "... because of the great honor which she has brought to our community and ... the great good which she has done through her community activities, I, Owen M. Begley mayor of the city of Schnectady, do hereby proclaim Wednesday, June 13, as Katharine B. Blodgett Day ... and I ask the people of the city to join in honoring this outstanding citizen. ..."

It is a tribute to Dr. Blodgett as a human being that even after she had become an internationally recognized authority in the field of surface chemistry, coworkers and friends still called her "Katie" and still got a kick out of her comic verses. They also chuckled over her attachment to the impossibly battered table and lab stool she'd used since joining the company in 1918. When the research staff moved into a sleek new facility, Dr. Blodgett insisted on bringing her old favorites along. Any effort to replace them was met with stubborn resistance.

After she retired in 1963, that well-used furniture became a treasured reminder of an unassuming woman named Katie who just happened to be one of the world's preeminent authorities in surface chemistry.

Dr. Katharine Blodgett died on October 12, 1979, at the age of eighty-one.

Chronology

January 10, 1898	Katharine Blodgett born in Schenectady, New York
1906	teachers note her ability in mathematics
1913	wins scholarship to Bryn Mawr
1916	tours General Electric laboratory at age of eighteen
1917	graduates from Bryn Mawr goes to University of Chicago
1918	writes thesis on absorption of gases by carbon earns M.S. degree becomes first woman scientist hired by General Electric
1924	begins doctoral studies at Cambridge
1926	becomes first woman to receive Ph.D. in physics from Cambridge
1933	begins experiments with monomolecular layers
December 1933	invents color gauge to measure thickness of monomolecular layers
December 1938	General Electric announces invention of nonreflective glass
1941	invents smokescreen for United States military
1951	Schenectady declares "Katharine Blodgett Day"
1963	retires from General Electric
October 12, 1979	dies at age of eighty-one

Further Reading

Macdonald, Anne L. *Feminine Ingenuity: Women and Invention in America*. New York: Ballantine Books, Inc., 1992. Feature on Dr. Blodgett.

O'Neill, Lois Decker. *Women's Book of World Records and Achievements*. Garden City, N.Y.: Anchor Press/Doubleday, 1979. Feature on Dr. Blodgett.

Vare, Ethlie Ann and Greg Ptacek. *Mothers of Invention*. New York: William Morrow and Co., 1988. Brief feature on Dr. Blodgett.

Yost, Edna. *American Women of Science*. Philadelphia, Penn.: Frederick A. Stokes Company, 1943. Section on Dr. Blodgett.

Elizabeth Hazen (1885–1975) and Rachel Brown (1898–1980)

Drs. Elizabeth Hazen (left) and Rachel Brown pose in front of their breakthrough formula.
(Courtesy Wadsworth Center Photo and Illustration Unit)

*T*he discovery of antibiotics, like many other breakthroughs in medicine, proved to be a two-edged sword. The "broad spectrum" antibiotics kill virtually all bacteria in their path, even beneficial ones such as those normally found in a healthy intestinal tract. Without these bacteria, an opportunistic fungal infection can wreck havoc on the patient's digestive system.

Elizabeth Hazen and Rachel Brown

Fungi are everywhere—in soils, in plants, in dark, moist places. They propagate by releasing microscopic spores into the surrounding environment. Fungal infections are responsible for a wide variety of conditions, from athlete's foot and ringworm to a potentially deadly lung infection that mimics tuberculosis.

In 1946, two dedicated scientists joined forces to combat these elusive infections. Elizabeth Lee Hazen and Rachel Fuller Brown made an excellent team through the long process that led to Nystatin, the first fungicide deemed safe for human use.

Elizabeth Lee Hazen was born on August 24, 1885, near the small farming town of Lula, Mississippi. Orphaned at the age of three, Elizabeth was raised by her aunt and uncle, Robert and Laura Hazen. They treated Elizabeth and her older sister, Annis, as full-fledged members of the family.

Robert Hazen believed in education. He became a trustee of the Lula School to ensure that it had capable teachers and a challenging curriculum. All of the Hazen children were good students, but Elizabeth was exceptional. She graduated from Lula School as valedictorian of her class and went on to the state-supported Mississippi Industrial Institute and College, (later, Mississippi State College for Women) where she earned her B.S. degree in 1910.

In college, Elizabeth Hazen was a 5-foot-tall dynamo whose ready wit softened her sometimes bossy manner. Though she had little interest in the flirtatious games of her husband-hunting contemporaries, she was surprisingly concerned about her personal appearance. She dressed attractively, always wore her hair in a fashionable style, and tended to the smallest details of grooming. Later in life, this concern for appearances turned into a hatred of birthdays; she wasn't above skipping a few when she filled out the vital statistics on employment applications and other documents.

Like many educated women of her time, Hazen found employment opportunities limited. For six years, she worked as a high school science teacher, taking advanced courses during summer breaks. In 1916, she moved to New York City, where she continued to mix work and graduate school. She received her Ph.D. in microbiology from Columbia University in 1927.

Four years later, Augustus Wadsworth of the New York State Department of Health offered her the job of a lifetime: heading the Bacterial Diagnosis Laboratory of the department's Division of Laboratories and Research. Rachel Brown had already been with the division for nearly five years. It would be seventeen years before the two scientists would meet to begin their historic collaboration.

Rachel Brown followed an equally roundabout route to that collaboration. Born November 23, 1898, in Springfield, Massachusetts, Rachel was the first child of George and Annie Brown. In childhood, she showed an artistic rather than scientific bent, preferring to study drawing and painting rather than chemistry and physics.

Rachel and younger brother Sumner had a life that was comfortable and normal until their father left the family. Rachel was in her last year of elementary school at the time. She had grown up expecting to go to high school and then to college; George Brown's exit put that future in jeopardy. High school wasn't free in 1910; students had to buy their books and sometimes pay tuition or laboratory fees.

Though family finances were uncertain, Annie Brown was a determined, high-spirited woman—determined that Rachel and Sumner would not be denied an education because they came from a fatherless home. She took a secretarial job at the Episcopal church in Springfield and supported not only her children but her aged parents as well.

Annie Brown's example had a great impact on her bright, academically gifted daughter. Rachel grew up with the role model of a woman who worked, achieved, and paid her own way in the world. Because of Annie's determination, Rachel went to high school as planned, graduating magna cum laude in 1916. She achieved this academic success while still managing to have a wide circle of friends and a reasonably active social life. Her easygoing demeanor revealed little of her inner determination to do something important with her life.

Rachel's big ambition as she finished high school was to attend prestigious Mount Holyoke College. That seemed to be an economic impossibility. Mount Holyoke cost $425 per year, a substantial sum at the time. She was investigating scholarships at other, less expensive, colleges when an old friend of the family stepped in to offer her a private scholarship. Henrietta Dexter agreed to pay Rachel's tuition and expenses at Mount Holyoke. All she asked in return was that the young woman live up to her obvious potential. This Rachel gladly promised to do.

It was at Mount Holyoke that Rachel Brown discovered the career path her life would follow. She took chemistry only because she needed a laboratory science in order to graduate, and it seemed like the least objectionable of the possible choices. To her complete surprise, she thrived on the challenge of peering into some unknown substance to separate and identify its various ingredients. By the end of the course, she couldn't imagine anywhere she'd rather be than in a chemistry laboratory. She promptly changed her major, and in 1920 received her A.B. degree in chemistry from Mount Holyoke.

At the urging of one of her professors, Rachel went to the University of Chicago for her graduate work. She taught in a girls high school and worked in an industrial laboratory to support herself while completing requirements for her doctorate. She submitted her thesis in 1926, but ran into a series of delays on the oral

> ❧ "Recently I had a severe shock. A high school girl who wanted to [study] biology was advised by her counselor not to do so because 'the opportunities are few for women.' It is hard to understand why the many life sciences should not offer just the right chances for women to express themselves. Consider Rachel Carson's *Silent Spring*. . . ."
>
> —Dr. Rachel Brown
> April 15, 1977

exam. After using up her savings waiting for a degree committee to assemble, she had no choice but to look for a job. On the
recommendation of a friend from Mount Holyoke, she applied
to the New York State Department of Health for a position in
the Division of Laboratories and Research.

The division was a state-of-the-art research facility, with a reputation for encouraging gifted scientists in their research efforts.
At the headquarters in Albany and the branch laboratory in New
York City, director Augustus Wadsworth created an atmosphere
where ideas—and people—could flourish and grow.

Part of that interest in division employees extended beyond
their job concerns. For example, Wadsworth knew about Rachel
Brown's Ph.D. problems. For nearly seven years, she'd been trying without success to assemble a degree committee at a time
when she could appear to take her orals. When the division
chose her to speak at an important scientific meeting in Chicago, Wadsworth saw the chance to help. He got in touch with her
thesis adviser and arranged for Brown to take her orals while
she was in the city for the conclave. She passed easily, returning
to Albany with her Ph.D. in organic chemistry and bacteriology.

The new doctor of science continued her research, seeking a
reliable method to identify the pathogens that caused pneu-
monia, which was still a major public health problem in those
days before sulfa drugs and penicillin. She also developed a
quick and reliable screening procedure for syphilis. Her simple
method detected suspicious blood samples in a fraction of the
time it would take to run a full analysis. Since 90% of samples
showed negative for the syphilis spirochete (bacteria), this
meant that only 10% would require the longer procedure.

In New York City, microbiologist Hazen was also involved in
testing. In her early years at the lab, she became something of
a microbiological detective, tracking outbreaks of contagious
illnesses to their source. She had a flair for this work, possibly
because she wasn't afraid to poke around in unlikely places.
One early assignment had her on the trail of a dangerous outbreak of anthrax, a usually fatal animal disease that can be
passed to humans. Instead of the usual cow pastures, barns,

and feed bins, she found the source of the infection in a brush factory with a contaminated supply of animal bristles.

Hazen was on the scene when the deadly botulism toxin made its first appearance in the United States. In a disciplined, intense effort, she tracked the infection to its source: canned fish imported from Germany and Labrador.

In 1944, Augustus Wadsworth gave Hazen a challenge worthy of her finely honed abilities: the fungus diseases. Wadsworth sensed that they would become increasingly important. There had been major outbreaks of fungal infections in Panama and the midwestern United States, and side effects of the broad-spectrum antibiotics were turning human intestinal tracts into breeding grounds for opportunistic fungi.

As the division had no mycologist (a scientist who studies fungi), Wadsworth assigned Elizabeth Hazen to become the resident expert in the field. She was well on her way to this goal when Augustus Wadsworth retired from the laboratory that would one day carry his name: Wadsworth Center, New York State Department of Health.

If Hazen wondered what would happen to her mycology project under a new director, Gilbert Dalldorf soon put her mind at ease. Like Wadsworth, he saw the importance of the work and the growing need for a safe and effective fungicidal drug. It was Dalldorf who brought Rachel Brown and Elizabeth Hazen together. In 1948, Hazen was gathering soil samples that showed evidence of antifungal activity, but she needed a biochemist to isolate the active agents involved. Brown had been working on a project to isolate antibacterial substances and

> ❦ "I have direct supervision of . . . a large number of technicians who are engaged in the examination of pathological specimens for the diagnosis of infectious diseases. . . . I supervise the work of the serum diagnosis department in which the complement-fixation test for syphilis is performed on thousands of blood and spinal fluid specimens."
> —Dr. Elizabeth Hazen

was using similar techniques to those that would be needed with Hazen's soil samples.

One day Dalldorf showed up in Brown's laboratory with a petite, energetic scientist who possessed an impish sense of humor and an obvious passion for her work. The collaboration that would produce Nystatin was soon under way.

Hazen had been collecting fungus cultures and soil samples since 1944, but as the project swung into high gear, she redoubled her efforts. Every colleague, friend, or casual acquaintance was prevailed upon to gather soil from as many different environments as possible. Hazen labeled each new offering with place of origin and name of donor and added it to her growing collection.

The testing procedure was simple but methodical. Hazen mixed a tiny amount of a sample into a sterile saline solution and placed it upon a nutrient base. When promising cultures grew large enough to be visible, she placed them on a growing fungus and observed the action. Those that stopped the growth were produced in larger quantities and shipped in mason jars to Albany, where Rachel Brown took over. Through a painstaking process of trial and error, Dr. Brown had to find a chemical solvent that would isolate the antifungal substance from the rest of the culture. These extracts went back to Dr. Hazen, who tested them against samples of two disease-causing fungi to see which ones would kill the organism or stop its growth. Several extracts looked promising but on further research proved to be too toxic for use in living creatures.

Then Elizabeth Hazen decided to visit friends who lived on a dairy farm in Virginia. From long habit, she gathered soil samples in various parts of the farm, patiently labeled each one, and took them with her back to New York. One of those samples yielded a microorganism like nothing Hazen had ever seen before. She named it *Streptomyces noursei* in honor of her hosts, the Nourse family, and proceeded to conduct the usual analysis. *Streptomyces noursei* passed every test. Not only did it destroy the two test fungi, but fourteen others as well, and animal testing indicated that it was only mildly toxic.

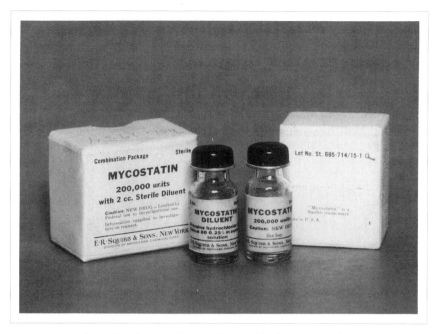

*Nystatin made medical news all over the world when it was first produced by
E.R. Squibb & Sons, under the brand name Mycostatin.*
(Courtesy Wadsworth Center Photo and Illustration Unit)

With cautious optimism, Brown and Hazen named the drug
Nystatin, in honor of New York State. They reported their preliminary findings to colleagues at the division, but hesitated to
"go public" until Nystatin had passed further trials.

Gilbert Dalldorf had other ideas. He saw that the research
was sound, and scheduled the scientists to present their findings at a meeting of the National Academy of Sciences on
October 10, 1950. Brown and Hazen were stunned; their notes
weren't in final form, they said. They couldn't possibly present
a coherent paper in so short a time. Dalldorf blithely assured
them that they could. In a wild flurry of activity, Brown and
Hazen organized their findings and went to the meeting.

Dalldorf assumed they would make a joint presentation, but
Elizabeth Hazen had other ideas. She adamantly refused to

appear on the podium, leaving the honor of delivering the paper to Rachel Brown. No one ever knew why she did this; she would never give a reason.

It certainly wasn't timidity. Elizabeth Hazen had never been afraid to speak her mind or deliver a small, fierce lecture if the occasion seemed to demand one. When an excited newspaper reporter practically grabbed the Nystatin paper from Rachel Brown's hands, Hazen brought him up short with a single withering glance. The drug was not perfected yet, she said, and warned against saying, or even hinting, that it was safe for human use.

The chastised reporter wrote a story that was suitably restrained, but still the announcement caused a minor sensation. Pharmaceutical companies began to call, asking about licensing rights, and the partners also had to face the dreaded patent process. Neither was prepared for these nonscientific complications. Much to their relief, Gilbert Dalldorf stepped in; as head of the division, he was accustomed to dealing with such matters.

Dalldorf contacted Research Corporation, a nonprofit foundation that specialized in developing academic inventions and channeling the income from them into support for future scientific research. The foundation handled the intricacies of the patenting process and licensed E.R. Squibb & Sons, a major pharmaceutical company, to produce and market the drug.

Squibb conducted the clinical trials, establishing that Nystatin was both safe and effective for human use. On January 25, 1957, Rachel Brown and Elizabeth Hazen received Patent No. 2,797,183, which they promptly assigned to Research Corporation. Over the years, the foundation received $13 million in royalties from Nystatin, using the money to fund research grants in scientific institutions all over the country. Neither Brown nor Hazen took anything from those earnings.

With success came honors, awards, and a good deal of media attention. Brown tolerated this fame with her usual equanimity. Hazen appreciated the professional honors but hated the media attention. She continued her long-standing refusal to present papers at scientific conferences and went to great lengths to dodge photographers intent on taking her picture.

Drs. Hazen and Brown received many professional honors for their work on Nystatin. In 1969, Hobart and William Smith

Hazen and Brown, shown here with Dr. Gilbert Dalldorf, at the presentation ceremony for the Squibb Award in Chemotherapy.
(Courtesy Wadsworth Center Photo and Illustration Unit)

Colleges in Geneva, New York, conferred honorary doctorates upon them. In 1975, they became the first women ever to win the prestigious Chemical Pioneer Award of the American Institute of Chemists. In a historic aside all her own, Dr. Hazen became the first non-chemist to win the award. The Institute had to change its bylaws to make her eligible. For Dr. Brown, perhaps the most personally satisfying award was an honorary doctorate from her alma mater, Mount Holyoke College, in 1972.

Both scientists took a strong interest in education in later life; Brown, as the division's representative on the State Health Department's training committee, and Hazen at Columbia, where she acted as a kind of mentor to promising students and gave guest lectures on mycology.

Elizabeth Hazen died on June 24, 1975, just a few weeks after she made history as the first female non-chemist to receive the Chemical Pioneer Award. She was eighty-nine. Rachel Brown died on January 14, 1980, at the age of eighty-two. In 1994, the two scientists were inducted into the National Inventors Hall of Fame, in recognition and memory of their ground-breaking achievement.

Chronology

August 24, 1885	Elizabeth Hazen born in Lula, Mississippi
1888	orphaned, goes to live with aunt and uncle
November 23, 1898	Rachel Brown born in Springfield, Massachusetts
1904	Hazen graduates from Lula School
1905	enrolls at Mississippi Industrial Institute and College
1910	Hazen receives B.S. degree
	begins teaching in Jackson, Mississippi
	Brown's father leaves the family
1916	Brown graduates from high school
	enters Mount Holyoke College
	Hazen leaves teaching to enter graduate school
1920	Brown graduates from Mount Holyoke
	begins graduate work at University of Chicago
1926	Brown submits her Ph.D. thesis
	begins working at Division of Laboratories and Research in Albany
1927	Hazen receives Ph.D. in microbiology from Columbia
1931	Hazen begins working for Division of Laboratories and Research branch laboratory in New York City
1933	Brown receives Ph.D. in organic chemistry and bacteriology from the University of Chicago
1944	Hazen begins study of mycology

1945	Brown begins development of screening test for syphilis
1948	Brown and Hazen begin their collaboration
October 10, 1950	announce invention of Nystatin
January 25, 1957	receive patent No. 2,797,183
1969	receive honorary doctorates from Hobart and William Smith Colleges in Geneva, New York
1972	Brown receives honorary degree from her alma mater, Mount Holyoke College
May 22, 1975	Hazen and Brown receive Chemical Pioneer Award of American Institute of Chemists
June 24, 1975	Elizabeth Hazen dies at age eighty-nine
January 14, 1980	Rachel Brown dies at age eighty-two
1994	Brown and Hazen inducted into the National Inventors Hall of Fame

Further Reading

Baldwin, Richard S. *The Fungus Fighters: Two Women Scientists and Their Discovery*. Ithaca, N.Y.: Cornell University Press, 1981. A thorough look at the lives and work of the two scientists.

Macdonald, Anne L. *Feminine Ingenuity: Women and Invention in America*. New York: Ballantine Books, 1992. Contains a short chapter on Hazen and Brown.

Vare, Ethlie Ann and Greg Ptacek. *Mothers of Invention*. New York: William Morrow and Co., 1988. Contains a brief feature on Hazen and Brown.

Bette Graham
(1924–1980)

Bette Graham not only invented Liquid Paper, but made her company a pleasant and creative place to work.
(Courtesy The Gillette Company)

*T*hroughout history, some of the most successful inventions have been those that solve common problems in uncommon ways. Transcription errors certainly qualify as a common problem; no doubt they've been with us since scribes first carved hieroglyphs into stone. Because someone invented the pencil, someone else had to invent the eraser. The fountain pen made ink eradication a minor necessity of life.

The electric typewriter required a whole new approach to error correction. On the older, manual machines, erasing had been difficult and time-consuming, but it was at least possible. With the carbon-film ribbons of the electrics, even careful erasing left a noticeable smudge. Secretaries all over the country bemoaned this unfortunate flaw. Bette Nesmith did something about it. She solved her problem with a small bottle of tempera paint and went on to create a multimillion-dollar business.

━━━━━━━

Bette Clair McMurray was born on March 23, 1924, in Dallas, Texas. Her father was an auto wholesaler, her mother a homemaker with an artistic flair. Bette was a high-spirited girl whom sister Yvonne described as "strong-willed and determined to do her own thing."

These qualities would serve Bette well in adulthood, but in her teens they caused trouble. Bette McMurray was something of a discipline problem for the school, and school was a distinct annoyance for her. She dropped out at the age of seventeen, determined to find a job and make her own way in the world.

Many girls in Bette's position would have aimed low, afraid they couldn't land anything but drudge-work. Bette marched into a prominent law firm and applied for a job as a secretary, even though she didn't know how to type. It was an audacious thing to do, but through some quirk of fate it paid off: the firm liked the bright, attractive youngster who wasn't afraid to put herself on the line. Not only did they hire her, but they sent her to secretarial school. On her own, Bette earned her high school diploma at night school.

Just a year after leaving high school for a law office, she married her "steady," Warren Nesmith. Their son, Michael, was born a year later, on December 30, 1943. Bette was nineteen years old.

She never had the secure married life that young women were taught to expect in 1943. Warren went off to fight in World War II, leaving his young wife to live as a single parent before the term "single parent" was even invented. For three years, Bette worked and took care of Michael. When Warren came home, things had changed. Bette and Warren weren't carefree high school sweethearts anymore, nor were they a functioning couple. The war had denied them the chance to deepen their relationship and make it comfortable. Only a few months after Warren came home, the marriage ended in divorce.

Bette built her life around the baby and her work. By 1951, she had worked her way up to executive secretary for W. W. Overton, chairman of the board of Texas Bank & Trust in Dallas. That was no small achievement; in the 1940s and 1950s, that was about as high as a woman could hope to advance in the world of business.

Accounts of how Bette Nesmith came to invent Liquid Paper usually characterize her as a terrible typist. That might not be entirely correct; more than likely, she was a victim of technological progress. In 1951, bad typists didn't make it to the executive suite. The first question any personnel officer asked a female applicant was "How fast can you type?" Many companies required applicants to take a test, which would be graded for speed and accuracy.

Nesmith's problem was the new electric typewriter she would use at Texas Bank & Trust. Manual typists learned to arch the fingers high over the keyboard and strike each letter crisply, with a fair amount of force. Electrics called for a different technique; the slightest touch depressed a key, and a small "stutter" of the fingers could result in errors. To make matters worse, Nesmith's new machine used a carbon-film ribbon instead of a fabric ribbon. Carbon ribbons gave an impression that was crisp, clean, and next to impossible to erase. Even the most painstaking attempt left a telltale smudge.

Secretaries everywhere shared Bette Nesmith's dilemma. Accuracy improved as they got used to the lighter touch of an electric, but erasing continued to be a problem. It was the perfect time to develop a new correction fluid.

The idea for Liquid Paper came when Nesmith was doing some freelance artwork, painting the bank window for the Christmas holidays. As she worked, she noticed that artists never erased mistakes, they just painted over them. Why couldn't typists do the same thing?

Nesmith took a small bottle of tempera paint and her watercolor brush to the office. The technique worked. Errors vanished quickly, neatly, without leaving a trace. Her boss didn't notice. For five years, the fluid was her little secret: "Since I was correcting my mistakes with it, I was quiet about it," she explained.

Word did get around, though. In 1956, Bette Nesmith filled her first order for "Mistake Out," as she called it then. Before long, every secretary in her building was using it, and a local office supply dealer suggested that she market it.

Nesmith hadn't seriously considered going into business; after the dealer's question, she could think about little else. The first step was to stake out her claim to the invention. She changed the name from Mistake Out to Liquid Paper and applied for a trademark, which would protect the name and logo. To protect the product itself, she would need a patent, and that was an expensive process. An attorney would charge $400 just to do the patent search. Considering Nesmith's financial situation at that time, it might as well have been $1 million. She decided to go ahead without the patent.

During this period, she not only established the foundation for a business, but set out to improve her product as well. She wanted the fluid to be thicker and faster-drying, so it would cover more efficiently without saturating the paper.

She couldn't afford to hire a chemist, so she decided to learn how to do the job herself. Some library research produced a basic formula for tempera paint; a chemistry teacher at her son's school showed her different ways to modify it. A man in a paint manufacturing company taught her how to grind and

❦ "As a young woman with a son to raise alone, I suffered greatly with extreme lack. I was a Christian Scientist and had tried to work this problem out by turning to God, but I never seemed to get anywhere until I was willing to humbly let go of my fear of, and dependency on, matter."

mix it. Several companies gave her samples of wetting agents and other chemicals.

Bette Nesmith did the rest in her kitchen, trying different combinations of pigment, wetting agents, and resins. When she was satisfied with the formula, she tried to interest IBM in marketing Liquid Paper. She put together a simple presentation, consisting of two letters: one that took fifteen minutes to type using an eraser for corrections, and another that took two and one-half minutes with Liquid Paper. A friend took it to IBM's advertising agency in New York, but all to no avail. IBM wasn't interested.

The young inventor stood at a crossroad. She could try to interest another large company in her product, make it herself, or give up altogether. Nesmith believed in Liquid Paper, but she knew that manufacturing and marketing it on her own would be a huge undertaking. She also knew she had to try.

Around that time, Nesmith had a dream: one clear, compelling image of a $700 invoice blowing in the wind. "I felt as if the dream were telling me to get busy," she said. She was already busier than most people would care to be—juggling a full-time job, single motherhood, and a fledgling business.

Much of the work was trial-and-error in those early days. Nesmith started out packaging her fluid in tubes with a felt applicator tip. Customers liked the convenience of this form, but Bette wasn't satisfied with the way it flowed. She finally discarded the tube in favor of the polyethylene bottle that would become a familiar sight in offices all over the world.

By the end of 1957, sales averaged 100 bottles per month and life at the Nesmith house was built around the business. Bette used the kitchen for making the fluid and the garage for filling containers. When she needed help to fill a batch of orders, she pressed her son Mike and his friends into service. In 1957, the kitchen smelled more like paint than meat loaf, and the garage was crowded with teenagers putting up bottles of Liquid Paper.

Nesmith found customers through the phone book, sending product sheets to local businesses and office supply dealers. In 1958, she sent press releases and product sheets to a number of trade publications, hoping that one of them might run an article about her correcting fluid.

In October, *The Office* mentioned Liquid Paper in its "New Products of the Month" feature. The response was much larger than Nesmith had dared to hope: 500 readers wrote to the magazine and hundreds more, directly to the company. In December, *The Secretary* published a short item that drew another flood of responses.

Nesmith scurried to keep up; she had product to make and bottle, orders to fill, and letters and invoices to write. Frequently, she worked all night on her own business, then reported to the office the next morning without any sleep. The stress was punishing, and finally it took an inevitable toll: Nesmith signed an important letter for her employer with the name of her own company. Though her work had always been good, she was fired for that mistake.

For the first time since starting her enterprise, Nesmith was truly on her own. Liquid Paper took more and more time, yet she still didn't earn enough to support the household. She found a part-time job to tide her over while she continued to build the business and improve the product. She was still not satisfied with the drying time of Liquid Paper, so she scraped up $200 to pay a chemist to develop a faster-drying formula. Liquid Paper was at last what she had wanted it to be all along.

Michael was seventeen by then, old enough to fend for himself for short periods. Nesmith began traveling around Texas, introducing office supply dealers to the merits of her product. One trip to San Antonio resulted in what was at the time a huge order—1 gross. A few weeks later, the dealer ordered another gross, and then another.

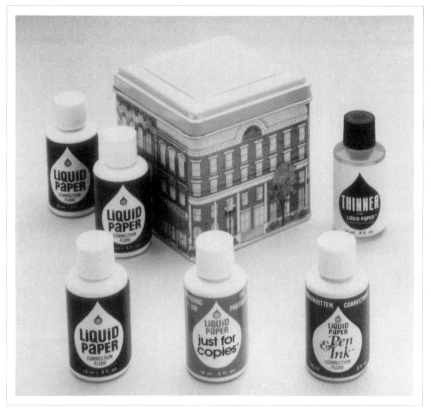

*From Bette Graham's first formula, the Liquid Paper Corporation diversified
its product line to suit a variety of needs.*
(Courtesy The Gillette Company)

By 1962, demand for the product had grown to the point
that Nesmith had two part-time employees earning $1 per hour
manufacturing and bottling Liquid Paper. With a $500 loan,
she bought a 10 × 26-foot portable building and set it up in her
backyard. Finally, the business moved out of the kitchen and
the garage and into quarters of its own.

Nesmith took pride in that humble little structure. With car-
pet, artwork, and hanging plants, she transformed half of it
into an office area. In the manufacturing section, she used
homemade curtains to hide the supplies stored under the

counters. The overall effect might not have been luxurious, but it was clean and cheerful, and it showed the attention to detail that marked everything Nesmith did.

Separating home from business was a milestone of sorts. For seven long years, Bette Nesmith's whole existence had revolved around Liquid Paper. The only personal life she allowed herself was her commitment to her son and her church. Then in 1962, Bette met and married Bob Graham, who soon came to share her involvement with the business.

Together, the Grahams traveled outside of Texas, calling on office supply dealers to leave a dozen bottles of Liquid Paper and a supply of brochures. In 1963, they set up a booth at the National Office Products Association Convention in Memphis. Many companies spend hundreds of dollars to create impressive displays at major trade shows. The Grahams gathered a plant, a typewriter, a chair from their dining room, and a painting borrowed from the public library. With the artistic ingenuity that had served her so well in the past, Bette created an attractive backdrop for her display. So it was that Liquid Paper made a credible debut among the "big boys" of the office supply business.

The next year, Bette Graham hired her first full-time employee; Judy Canup, who had already been working part time, became office manager. More employees followed. Unfortunately, each stage of expansion raised expenses as well as earnings. To fill the growing number of orders, the company needed bigger facilities, better machinery, and more workers. Graham had always insisted on a high standard of quality, regardless of cost. She wasn't about to relax that standard. In the long run, quality would tell; Bette Graham believed that with all her heart.

By 1966, son Michael had moved to Los Angeles and become part of the Monkees, a four-man pop group with its own television show and a hit tune, "I'm a Believer." At least one writer estimated that twenty-three-year-old Michael Nesmith earned more that year than the entire Liquid Paper company.

> ❧ "In ten years we have come from production in a kitchen . . . to a corporation employing many people. . . . There have been many facets to our success . . . the ability to see a right idea . . . the stamina to work and the intelligence to plan . . . the faith to [measure progress] by the good accomplished."
> —Excerpt from Bette Graham's speech at 1968 company meeting

Growth continued, however, and at a steadily accelerating pace. By the end of the 1960s, Bette Graham's brainchild was grossing more than $1 million per year on domestic sales, and Graham was looking to expand into the international market. The company moved to a spacious new headquarters in 1968, where automated equipment turned out sixty bottles of Liquid Paper per minute. In the first year of automation, the company sold 1 million bottles of correction fluid. Two years later, the figure was up to 5 million bottles.

Each step in the process moved the company farther away from Bette Graham's direct control. The Liquid Paper Corporation became an entity in its own right, with its own organizational needs, its own identity. Graham became "the founder" and then "chairman of the board." These were not titles that belonged to a visionary inventor or a hands-on entrepreneur. These were organizational titles that came from the executive suite.

With typical grace, Bette Graham adapted to the change. Instead of trying to preserve her own power and singular status within the company, she set up a plan to give everyone a voice in day-to-day operations. In the business environment of the early 1970s, Graham's ideas were fresh, innovative, and even a bit strange. By the 1980s, American executives would know it as "Japanese-style management."

Bette Graham didn't really have a name for it; she only knew that she wanted everyone who worked at Liquid Paper to feel like an important member of the team. "Each employee's contribution was regarded as equal in importance and value," she once told an interviewer for the *Christian Science Journal*.

Secretaries, vice presidents, and production people served together on a variety of planning committees. There were groups for new product development, marketing strategies, office operations, manufacturing techniques—virtually every facet of the operation. The committees gathered regularly to brainstorm ideas, refine the best ones into workable strategies, and propose them to the executive committee. After a few years more growth, the committee structure became unwieldy and was discontinued. Everyone who had been part of it, though, remembers it with fondness. For a company that was busy transforming itself from cottage industry to international corporation, the concept was both effective and inspiring.

In 1975, Liquid Paper Corporation remodeled its headquarters building to reflect the company's growing international standing. People who knew Bette Graham saw her hand in the design. She wanted the building to be an "environmental art form," with spans of gleaming glass, triangular shapes, and richly contrasting textures. Inside, paintings and sculptures brightened the lobby, the hallways, and even the manufacturing areas. Outside, a beautifully landscaped greenbelt featured a goldfish pool and an elegant birdcage containing twenty finches.

The headquarters building was one of Bette Graham's last projects for the company she founded. She resigned as chairman of the board in 1976, to devote herself to her religion and a number of charities she had supported over the years. In 1979, her "little" company became part of the Gillette Corporation. When Graham died on May 12, 1980, the onetime secretary left a multimillion-dollar fortune, which was, as she had willed, divided equally between her son and her charitable foundations.

> "The building was a beautiful vehicle for communication. It communicated to the world what Liquid Paper Corporation was—that we had vision, that we had style, that we felt an obligation to our employees, that we were confident about our future, that we were interested in quality and excellence."

Chronology

March 23, 1924	Bette Clair McMurray born in Dallas, Texas
1941	drops out of high school to take a job
1942	marries high school sweetheart Warren Nesmith
December 30, l943	son Michael born
1946	divorces Warren Nesmith
1951	gets a new job—and a new electric typewriter
	creates her first correction fluid
1956	sells fluid to other secretaries
	researches better formula
	offers newly named Liquid Paper to IBM
1958	fired for typing her own company name on a letter for her employer
1962	marries Bob Graham
1968	company moves to new headquarters
1972	begins opening international markets
1975	headquarters enlarged and remodeled into an "environmental art form"
1976	Bette Graham resigns to devote her time to charity and spiritual pursuits
1979	Gillette buys Liquid Paper
May 12, 1980	Bette Graham dies in Dallas, Texas

Further Reading

O'Neill, Lois Decker. *Women's Book of World Records and Achievements*. Garden City, N.Y.: Anchor Press/Doubleday, 1979. Includes a section on Bette Graham.

Vare, Ethlie Ann and Greg Ptacek. *Mothers of Invention*. New York: William Morrow and Co., 1988. Includes a section on Bette Graham.

Ruth Handler
(1916–   )

Ruth Handler, designer of Barbie and co-founder of Mattel.
(Courtesy Mattel, Inc. ©1996. Mattel, Inc.)

Mass or "pop" culture as we know it today is largely a product of modern technology, and therefore, of inventors who created that technology or devised new ways to use it. Popular culture includes those things that cut across social class, ethnic origin, and geographic location to reach millions of people simultaneously. Everything from pulp magazines and tabloid newspapers to movies, radio, television, and recorded music is part of America's pop culture. So are toys.

The toy business is notoriously prone to fad and fashion. One season, every child in America absolutely has to have the latest battery-operated robot. Next season, it's a working model of the lunar lander or a game based on a new Saturday morning cartoon. Sometimes a toy outlasts fashion to become a pop culture classic, beloved by several generations of children.

The Barbie doll is such a toy. When Barbie first appeared in 1959, many industry experts didn't think she'd last for the rest of the season, much less the rest of the century. She was a grown-up doll with grown-up clothes and a full-breasted figure. Such a doll would never sell, they said; little girls wanted to play at being mothers, and you couldn't do that with an adult doll. No, said Ruth Handler, the woman who created Barbie and brought her to market; little girls wanted to play at being bigger girls.

Handler's instincts were right. By the mid-1990s, sales topped $1 billion worldwide, and the typical American girl between the ages of three and ten owned an average of eight Barbies. Ruth Handler has moved on to other things, but millions of girls will always remember her for bringing Barbie into their lives.

Ruth Mosko was born in Denver, Colorado, on November 4, 1916. She was the tenth and last child of Jacob and Ida Moskowicz who had fled Poland to make a new life in the United States. Jacob had arrived in 1907; Ida and their six oldest children followed one year later. Somewhere along the line, the family name got shortened from Moskowicz to Mosko.

Ida Mosko was forty when she bore her last child, and the years of unrelenting work had taken their toll. Just six months after Ruth was born, Ida had to have gallbladder surgery. Eldest daughter Sarah and her new husband Louie Greenwald agreed to care for the baby. In time, and without anybody saying a great deal about it, an emergency arrangement became a permanent one. Ruth kept close ties with her parents, but she lived with Sarah and Louie.

The couple owned a drugstore across the street from Denver General Hospital. By the time Ruth was ten, she was spending most of her afternoons there, waiting on customers, working the cash register, and even serving soft drinks and sandwiches at the soda fountain. The Greenwalds didn't force her to work; Ruth wanted to do it. The drug store provided some of the fondest memories of Ruth's childhood.

The happiest memories of her teen years were mostly linked to a young man she had first seen on her sixteenth birthday. Isadore Elliot Handler was a struggling art student from the wrong side of town when he and Ruth fell in love. The Greenwalds tried to break it up; Elliot was too poor to support a wife, they said, and his prospects for the future were far from bright.

When Ruth was nineteen, she moved to Los Angeles to work in the steno pool at Paramount Studios. Sarah and Louie were delighted that the job would take her away from Denver—and Elliot Handler. To their dismay, Elliot moved to Los Angeles a month later. His official reason for being there was to study industrial design at the Art Center School of Design. His ulterior motive was to be near Ruth. They were finally married on June 26, 1938.

Less than a year later, they started their first business. It began with an Art Center assignment to create household items from the new acrylic plastic, Lucite. Elliot made bookends, trays, candle holders, and the like. Ruth was so impressed with his designs that she felt sure she could sell them. In May of 1939, she left Paramount during her lunch hour, armed with her own sense of purpose and a suitcase full of samples.

She marched into an exclusive shop that catered to decorators and architects and came out with a $500 order. That was the beginning of the Handlers' first company, Elzac, formed by blending Elliot's name with that of the man who became a partner in the business, Zachary Zemby.

The Handlers' daughter Barbara was born in May 1941, son Kenneth in March 1944. As the children came, Ruth learned that being a stay-at-home mom just wasn't her style. She wanted to go back into the business world, but finding the right place to do it was a problem. Elzac was prospering without her; she didn't have the training for an executive position, and she didn't have the temperament to be a file clerk or a typist.

Opportunity came when Elliot and his friend Harold "Matt" Matson both decided to quit Elzac and strike out in new directions. Ruth joined them to form a new company. In what was becoming a Handler tradition, the partners combined syllables from two names to make a third: in this case, "Matt" and "el" became Mattel.

> ❧ "By the time Kenny was six months old, I had to admit it to myself; I was becoming increasingly restless at home. Domestic chores bored me silly. I missed the fast-paced business world and the adrenaline rush that came with closing a tough sale and delivering a gigantic order on time."

Mattel started out selling dollhouse furniture, not because the Handlers wanted to go into the toy business, but simply because the pieces could be fashioned from scrap materials. It was 1944—wartime—and many materials were in short supply. The ability to use what others threw away was a tremendous asset. Elliot and Matt produced the tiny, well-crafted pieces, and Ruth sold them to retailers.

It was touch and go in those early days: scraping for money and supplies, fighting price wars with other manufacturers. Matt soon found the life of an entrepreneur too risky for his taste. He sold his interest to Ruth's sister Sarah and her husband, then disappeared from the Handlers' lives. Ruth and Elliot settled into their customary division of labor; she handled marketing and management, he did product design.

Ruth Handler didn't become an inventor in her own right until the early 1950s, when she noticed something interesting in the way her daughter played with paper dolls. With hun-

> 🐞 "I was—I *am*—a fiercely independent woman, one who has always felt the need to prove myself, even when I was just a child."

dreds of different designs available, ten-year-old Barbara and her friends always chose adult female paper dolls. They had no interest in baby dolls or those of children close to their own age. With the adult figures, they fantasized themselves as grown-up women: wearing glamorous clothes, doing interesting things. What if they could do this with a three-dimensional doll? Ruth envisioned a grown-up young lady with nail polish, makeup—and a bustline. Nobody else liked the idea.

Then in the summer of 1956, the Handler family went to Europe for a working vacation. On a shopping trip in Lucerne, Switzerland, Ruth Handler saw "Lilli"; an 11½-inch doll with a figure out of men's fantasies and a hard, world-weary face.

Lilli was not a children's toy; she was an adult novelty. German cartoonist Reinhard Beuthien created her in a comic strip as an audacious golddigger with champagne tastes and no scruples about pursuing wealthy men for their money. The comic strip came out in 1952, the doll in 1955. Handler bought two Lillis that day: one for daughter Barbara, who loved the intricate ski outfit the doll was wearing, and one for herself, to prove a point.

From that time on, she was relentless. The doll she had in mind would work, she was sure of it; when Ruth Handler was sure of herself, she didn't let anything stand in her way. Lilli was an inspiration, not a model; Handler envisioned something softer, more wholesome. It took three years to design and produce the 11½-inch doll with the blonde ponytail and the knockout figure. Handler called it "Barbie," in honor of her own daughter.

Barbie made her debut on March 9, 1959, at the industry-wide Toy Show in New York City. Each year, toy manufacturers from all over the country gathered to present their new offerings to the wholesalers and retailers who could make or break

*The original 1959 Barbie, with her grown-up figure and striped bathing suit,
was an instant hit with the public.*
(Courtesy Mattel, Inc. © 1996. Mattel, Inc.)

a new toy. Handler expected great things from her brainchild. To her chagrin, half the buyers wanted nothing to do with Barbie. The rest placed relatively small, trial orders.

All that changed when the public got involved. Orders and reorders flooded Mattel's offices. For three years, demand exceeded production, and Mattel played a highly profitable game of catch-up. "Ken"—named for the Handler's son, Kenneth—made his debut in 1961, after thousands of little girls had written to say that Barbie needed a boyfriend.

Other dolls followed: a sister, a cousin, assorted friends and *their* boyfriends. Barbie's clothes were inspired by the fashion designers of the day, her activities by the latest crazes. In the early 1960s, she could go to the malt shop or the prom. In the 1970s, it was the disco. Barbie and her friends even had the costumes, scripts, and stage settings to put on seven different plays. For Barbie, life was one long party; for her creator, it was more difficult.

As a woman functioning in what was then regarded as a man's world, Handler sometimes drew criticism for traits that would have been accepted, or even admired, in a male executive: she was "too ambitious" or "too aggressive," "too persistent" or "too blunt." Despite such criticisms, even Ruth Handler's detractors admitted that she had a rare genius for business. Mattel soared to the top of the toy industry, and Barbie became a legend in her own time.

In the late 1960s, the Handlers began to realize that Mattel's phenomenal growth could not continue with new product development alone. There was a ceiling somewhere, and sooner or later, they would hit it. In 1966, after more than twenty years in business, Mattel reached $100 million in sales. Just three years later, that figure had doubled to $200 million. Nobody could keep that up indefinitely.

The Handlers decided to begin an expansion program, buying companies in allied fields to extend Mattel's base beyond the toy industry. They hired a specialist in corporate acquisitions to manage this new program. Later, Ruth would consider the whole idea a terrible mistake, but at the time she wasn't focusing on Mattel's future; she was thinking about her own.

In June of 1970, she was diagnosed with breast cancer and underwent a modified radical mastectomy to remove her left breast. The surgery left her scarred physically and emotionally depressed by this violation of her body. To add insult to injury, she couldn't find a decent prosthesis (artificial breast, worn by mastectomees).

The only prosthesis then on the market was what Handler described as "an egg-shaped *glob*" that fit into the pocket of a special surgical brassiere. It had strange sizing and an even stranger odor—something sharp and medicinal that clung to the wearer like an unwanted perfume. Handler wore a 36C bra, which meant she needed a size 5 or maybe a size 6 prosthesis— the fitter wasn't sure. The whole fitting process was shrouded in secrecy, as if it was shameful in some mysterious way.

Like other women before her, Handler hid behind layers of clothing, and put up with a prosthesis that was woefully inadequate to its purpose. Then she decided to do something about it. She went to Santa Monica to see Peyton Massey, a skilled craftsman who specialized in making artificial body parts. Putting her inventor's mind to the problem, she worked with Massey to design a truly effective artificial breast.

The result of that early experiment wasn't perfect by any means, but it was an enormous improvement over anything available on the market. Handler began to think about transforming her personal project into a business. There were thousands of women who needed a new kind of artificial breast. Why not create one they could wear with confidence?

The question intrigued Handler, but before she could do anything about it, she became embroiled in an increasingly difficult situation at Mattel. The company was growing into a hydra-headed creature the Handlers could no longer control. The offices that had been so friendly and easygoing became tense and riddled with intrigues. The young executives of the corporation moved ahead without the Handlers, not even bothering to keep them informed about what was going on within the company structure. By 1975, Ruth had all she could take. With great sadness,

Ruth Handler turned personal tragedy into a product that improved life for thousands of mastectomy patients. Here, she displys the first version of her Nearly Me breast prosthesis.
(Courtesy Nearly Me Mastectomy Products)

and not a little anger, she quit the company that she and her husband had founded. Elliot followed about six months later.

Once free of Mattel, Ruth went through another personal crisis. For several months, she was depressed and uncertain.

Elliot fulfilled a youthful dream and went back to art school. Ruth didn't know what to do with herself, until she began to think about the prosthesis again. In her usual direct and often dramatic way, she marched into Peyton Massey's office and informed him that she was "going into the breast business."

After years of experience at Mattel, her creative skills were finely honed. She proceeded with classic inventive strategy: identify the problem, decide what sort of device would best solve it, then figure out a way to make that device.

Handler had covered step one from hard experience, and her earlier work with Massey had given her some excellent ideas for producing a

> ❧ ". . . the most gratifying memories . . . from my sixteen years with Nearly Me are the many times . . . I stood toe to toe in fitting rooms with women I was really helping. Some came in hunched over, wearing baggy blouses. . . . Some came in depressed, confused, self-pitying. I'd fit them, and sometimes they would cry when they saw how Nearly Me had restored their looks."

superior breast form. It would be naturally shaped, lightweight, tightly fitted against the chest wall, and worn with a standard bra rather than a surgical one. In addition to all this, it should be mass-producible in a variety of standard bra sizes and be available in separate lefts and rights.

Peyton Massey thought it was impossible to create such a prosthesis; Handler convinced him otherwise. She gathered the best team of experts she could find—designers, chemists, materials and tooling experts—and set them to work on the problem. She and Massey did the modeling.

By January 1977 the "Nearly Me" breast prosthesis was ready for the market. Handler turned her attention from product development to promotion and advertising. She decided two things: Nearly Me would be sold by trained fitters only, and the atmosphere surrounding the purchase of an artificial breast would no longer be secretive and funereal. She went on television interview shows to talk frankly about breast cancer, mastectomy, and her reasons for designing a new prosthesis. She even posed for a picture with her blouse open and bra showing, daring anyone to tell which breast was which.

Handler felt good about Nearly Me, and about her second role as inventor-cum-entrepreneur. She arranged showings at upscale department stores, trained fitters in the proper techniques, and continued as an advocate for breast cancer survivors.

In 1991, Handler developed a heart problem that required surgical repair. As she would later say, the illness reminded her of her own mortality. After sixteen years of building Nearly Me into a respected product, she sold the company and stepped aside. She was seventy-five years old, with an up-again-down-again, roller-coaster career behind her. It was time to retire.

Retirement for Ruth Handler didn't mean a rocking chair and orthopedic shoes. She was still a public figure, often called upon to give interviews or make personal appearances. In 1994, Handler did something she thought she'd never do: she got involved with Mattel again. The management had changed in the years since her departure; Mattel had a personable young president in Jill Barad and a capable team of people who seemed to enjoy the business as much as Handler and her associates once had. Besides, it was the year that Barbie turned 35; a momentous event by anyone's standards.

Handler toured the country on a special anniversary promotion; Mattel brought out a faithful replica of the 1959 Barbie; and toy stores everywhere honored the doll that had become an American icon. March 9, the day that Barbie made her debut at the 1959 Toy Show, is considered her official birthday. Handler celebrated the occasion with an appearance at the famous F.A.O. Schwartz toy store in New York City, signing autographs and listening to people's most cherished Barbie memories. It was hectic, it was crowded, it was unabashedly sentimental; Ruth Handler enjoyed every noisy minute.

Chronology

November 4, 1916	Ruth Mosko born in Denver, Colorado
1926	begins working at sister's drugstore
1936	moves to California, works at Paramount Studios
1938	marries Elliot Handler
May 1939	begins selling Elliot's designs
1940	forms Elzac with Elliot and Zachary Zemby
May 1941	daughter Barbara born
March 1944	son Kenneth born
1944	forms Mattel with Elliot and Harold "Matt" Matson sells dollhouse furniture
1947	launches Mattel's first big hit, the Uke-A-Doodle
1949	Mattel produces full line of musical toys
1956	discovers "Lilli" in Lucerne, Switzerland designs "Barbie"
March 9, 1959	Barbie makes her debut at Toy Show
1961	"Ken" doll appears
1967	becomes president of Mattel
June 16, 1970	has mastectomy
1975	leaves Mattel
1976	designs "Nearly Me" artificial breast
1991	sells Nearly Me company and retires
March 9, 1994	appears at F.A.O. Schwartz to celebrate Barbie's thirty-fifth birthday

Further Reading

Handler, Elliot. *The Impossible Really Is Possible: The Story of Mattel*. New York: Newcommen Society, 1968. Handler's thoughts during the glory days.

Handler, Ruth, with Jacqueline Shannon. *Dream Doll: The Ruth Handler Story*. Stamford, Conn.: Longmeadow Press, 1994. A frank and readable autobiography that captures something of Handler's dynamic personality.

Lord, M. G. *Forever Barbie: The Unauthorized Biography of a Real Doll*. New York: William Morrow and Co., 1994. An outsider's view of Mattel, the Handlers, and the Barbie phenomenon.

Index

Boldface page numbers indicate main topics.
Italic page numbers indicate illustrations or captions.
Page numbers followed by *c* indicate chronology.

Index

Index